Letters from Artists in the Nineteenth Century

Letters from Artists in the Nineteenth Century

JOSEPH DARRACOTT

1997

First published in 1997
by Deirdre McDonald Books
7 Westhorpe Road
London SW15 1QH

ISBN 1 898094 08 X

Designed by Mick Keates

Phototypeset by Intype, London Ltd

Printed and bound in Great Britain
by Biddles Ltd

FOR BRITT-MARIE

My thanks to my family, colleagues and friends for various sorts of advice and help, and in particular my gratitude to Michael Darracott, Erika Langmuir, Kenneth McConkey and Alex Potts.

Contents

Acknowledgements

The author and publisher would like to thank the following for permission to use letters and extracts:

A & C Black (Publishers) Ltd, *Victorian Sidelights: from the papers of the late Mrs Adams-Acton*, A.M.W. Stirling, published by Ernest Benn, 1954.

Christopher and Elisabeth Thornycroft and The Henry Moore Institute, *Marble and Bronze: the art and life of Hamo Thornycroft*, by E. Manning, published 1982. Presented by Elfrida Manning to The Centre for the Study of Sculpture, Henry Moore Institute, Leeds.

By permission of Oxford University Press: Legge, Sylvia *Affectionate Cousins: T. Sturge Moore and Marie Appia*, 1980. © Sylvia Legge 1980; Gage, John (ed) *Collected Correspondence of J. M. Turner*, 1980. © John Gage 1980.

Reed Consumer Books Ltd, *Eugene Delacroix: Selected Letters 1813–1864*, trans. Jean Stewart, published by Eyre & Spottiswoode (1971).

Suffolk Records Society, *John Constable's Correspondence*, vol 2, R. B. Backett (ed), 1964.

Thames and Hudson Ltd, *Letters of the Great Artists, R. Friedenthal* (ed), published 1963.

The University of Chicago Press, *Letters of Gustave Courbet*, Chu, P. (ed), published 1992.

The University of Glasgow, French & German Publications for *Le Chauve-Souris et le Papillon*, J. Newton (ed), published 1990.

Yale Univerity Press, *From the Classicists to the Impressionists*, E. G. Holt (ed), 1966.

Although every effort has been made to contact all copyright holders, the publishers would be pleased to hear from anyone they have been unable to trace.

Introduction

Thousands of letters were written by artists during the nineteenth century. The number of artists grew as national populations increased; but this was not the only reason for a swollen volume of correspondence; it was largely due to the intelligent reforming principles of Sir Rowland Hill, inventor of the penny post. Prepaid postage and a standard rate for whatever distance a letter was sent were money-making policies for governments, which assumed control of a lucrative business. More efficient means of transport added to the attractions of postal systems, which created on the way to greater profits such things as postage stamps, picture postcards, Valentine cards and Christmas cards, which, incidentally, needed to be drawn by artists.

This anthology of around a hundred letters and extracts will raise expectations in the minds of readers. There are several celebrated letter writers who can be expected to appear, since they describe their aims in art with such compelling skill, and so Constable, Delacroix and van Gogh are not forgotten. Some letters are well known to students of art, though not by such prolific letter writers; a few of these are included, among them letters by Géricault, Millet, and Seurat. Too many well-known passages, however, would make a dull and superfluous book, and so a particular pattern of choice has been used.

The careers of nineteenth-century artists had a variety of shapes. Choosing letters to demonstrate the stages of artists' lives has been the principle on which this anthology is based; not every sort of career is represented, but the wheel of the century's fortune turns through the selection; different experiences of education lead on to a wide range of professional activities, some culminating in honours and great fortunes, some modest careers enriched by friendships or blighted by debts or disease, and a number of tragedies. Artists meet with Tzar Alexander, Queen Victoria or Gladstone; there are literary friendships, for example with Dickens or Tolstoy, family life for Friedrich or Constable can be glimpsed in vignette, and there is a passage about Rosa Bonheur's private zoo.

Let me say a word or too about the process of editing, since everything here has already been published, although not necessarily in English. A strict academic editor would print every letter as it was written, make explicit the extent of omissions, besides annotating all obscure references. My general rule has been to print letters as they have been found in my sources, which are listed. I have not always made clear where omissions occur. Sometimes this anthology gives more notes than the source, say a nineteenth-century edition, sometimes less, say in a recent edition. The notes are intended to be helpful, but are not comprehensive. As for spelling, sometimes unorthodox, at times English and at others American, I have eliminated comments drawing attention to it; the source has decided. Hence anyone wishing to quote a letter should check the source, not this edition designed, as a benign rubric has it, 'to be read as literature'.

For letters are literature, and may be so enjoyed. Not everything here counts high on the literary scale, certainly not letters of business or the memorandum addressed by Dahl to a Minister. On the other hand, letters written privately and those written for publication sometimes come close together in style, as Ruskin demonstrates. We are looking back at a century when sermons, lectures, and novels can have an epistolary tincture, even a letter form. In some of the chapter introductions I have inserted passages from novels by Hawthorne and Zola to set the scene. Diary passages have been rather avoided, even if there are some brief exceptions, since the diary has a literary life of its own.

Nothing can match the best sort of letters, which, as the poet William Walsh said, 'ought to be free, easy and natural; as near approaching to familiar conversation as possible'.

1
EDUCATING THE ARTIST

'Education alone can make the artist; and by education I mean the complete acquisition of those intellectual powers on which imagination feeds, the full development of those moral qualities which afford a key to feeling and passion, and such an experience of social laws as may result in an apprehension of the needs of man and in the power of giving them expression.

For this is the sole aim of art. It expands at the summit of a phase of civilization as a flower does at the summit of a plant which has long been nourished through its roots underground, through its stems and leaves above ground. The flower is the outcome of these long, slow efforts.'[1]

This pronouncement by Ernest Chesnau touches on most of the issues which by 1863 deeply concerned planners of art programmes; furthermore, social divisions in society, it was felt, needed to be attacked; ' "What is to be done?" The reader is prepared with the answer: "The development of the illiterate classes, by giving them scientific and literary training, must be carried out simultaneously with the improved artistic training of the cultured classes".'[1]

At the beginning of the century the education of the artist had not been seen in such organisational terms. Schools of art existed but these were only slowly emerging from the pattern of patronage and earlier arrangements of teaching apprentices or at Academies, of which the developing Royal Academy of Arts in London can be given as an example. Where to study was an important question, and remained so throughout the century. At the end of the century Paris was a major attraction, but earlier, since classical art was so highly valued, Rome was the magnet for students.

The allure of Rome in the middle of the century is captured in *The Marble Faun*, Nathaniel Hawthorne's novel, which has a sculptor called Kenyon as one of the characters. Here is a description of his studio:[2]

> Kenyon's studio was in a cross-street, or, rather, an ugly and dirty little lane, between the Corso and the Via di Ripetta; and though chill, narrow, gloomy, and bordered with tall and shabby structures, the lane was not a whit more disagreeable than nine-tenths of the Roman streets. Over the door of one of the houses was a marble tablet, bearing an inscription, to the purport, that the sculpture-rooms within had formerly been occupied by the illustrious artist Canova. In these precincts (which Canova's genius was not quite of a character to render sacred, though it certainly made them interesting) the young American sculptor had now established himself.

A young painter and compatriot called Miriam comes to visit him there, and asks to see his new statue.

> 'Not a nude figure, I hope!' observed Miriam. 'Every young sculptor seems to think that he must give the world some specimen of indecorous womanhood, and call it Eve, Venus, a Nymph, or any name that may apologise for a lack of decent clothing. I am weary, even more than I am ashamed, of seeing such things. Now-a-days, people are as good as born in their clothes, and there is practically not a nude being in existence. An artist, therefore, – as you must candidly confess, – cannot sculpt nudity with a pure heart, if only because he is compelled to steal guilty glimpses at hired models. The marble inevitably loses its chastity under such circumstances. An old Greek sculptor, no doubt, found his models in the open sunshine, and among pure and princely maidens, and thus the nude statues of antiquity are as modest as violets, and sufficiently draped in their own beauty. But as for Mr. Gibson's coloured Venuses, (stained, I believe, with tobacco-juice,) and all other nudities of

> today, I really do not understand what they have to say to this generation, and would be glad to see as many heaps of quick-lime in their stead!'

As a taste for classical art retreated, so other interests, especially in nature and landscape, advanced. Paris gained its special prominence, though there was competition from other capitals; and it would be well to remember the internationalism of art during a century in which there were continual advances in the speed and means of transport.

Artists' letters about their education are unluckily more sparse than we could wish. Letters home are more inclined to record new experiences and fresh impressions in a strange city than to focus on instruction in the studios. We do not lack information about artistic education, but much of it is derived from autobiogaphies or other publications, apart from the administrative detail which can be disinterred from official documents. More individual training as an apprentice can be found in a few letters; it was the road to competence for an engraver, and could be used by a sculptor, as Harriet Hosmer's case demonstrates. For painters, technical training was important in a century where innovations in pigments and materials were being made. There was also the question of training in observation, carried out in academies through slow progress by studying from casts before working from live models, and an emphasis on the value of making copies. And there were variations, among them the remarkably successful method of Lecoq de Boisbaudran, praised by Horace Vernet.

Professional training for an artist, however, also involved other sorts of learning. It was rare for an artist to be a classical scholar, as Henry Fuseli was, but classical or literary references were required in much high art. While a polite education was the birthright of artists born into the middle classes, artists from humbler beginnings, as Chesnau pointed out, needed help. Delacroix may have been the son of an ambassador (or perhaps Talleyrand?), but Turner was definitely the son of a barber; Whistler was well born and entered the military academy at West Point as a cadet, but Herkomer was of Bavarian peasant stock. It was one of the roles of education to balance out social inequalities.

Finally, general knowledge of current events became essential for a new category of artist, the reporter for illustrated papers or magazines. Illustrators or cartoonists often had training in art schools; for example, although George Du Maurier originally hoped for success and fame as a fine artist, there is no doubt that his abilities were admirably suited to drawing for *Punch*. An illustrator's education could be widened by adventurous experiences, such as those of war correspondents, even if for others like Du Maurier, their lives were more tranquil.

Artistic centres

Cornelius in Rome

Peter von Cornelius arrived in Rome in 1811. The painters he describes in this letter were the Nazarenes, members of the Order of St Luke to which Cornelius was an eager recruit. Their ambition to paint together as if in a German medieval workshop was fulfilled after 1815, when they were commissioned to paint a fresco cycle of Joseph and his brethren. Two scenes of this successful project were assigned to Cornelius. His enhanced reputation resulted in a recall to Germany in 1819 by King Ludwig I of Bavaria.

This letter to a fellow artist starts with a reference to Cologne cathedral, whose original plans were found in 1814, leading to its completion during the century. The Nibelung sequence mentioned was successfully published in a series of engravings.

(to Carl Mossler)[3] Rome, March, 1812

. . . What you told me about the painting in the cathedral was a real comfort to me. Here, apart from the brothers of the cloister, one hears German art spoken of only with a certain politeness, which is especially distressing to me, since only here in Italy its nature in its true glory first appeared to me and becomes ever dearer to me. I tell you, Mossler, and I really believe it, a German painter should not go away from his fatherland. I have taken this step against time, and in this way it is good, but I do not want to live long under this warm sky, where hearts are so cold. With pain and joy I feel I am a German to the core. However, one cannot deny that there is much art material to be obtained here, although also much is seductive, and indeed the most refined is in Raphael himself. In his art, more than I ever thought possible, lies the greatest poison and the true spirit of rebellion and protestantism. One would like to weep tears of blood when one sees that a spirit, who saw the Almighty even as that mighty angel at the throne of God, that such a spirit could become faithless. More on this point another time; now a word about the brothers of the cloister. They are a company of very excellent people who, for art and everything good, have united and who love one another and are attached to one another. There are six of them, five here and one in Vienna. Overbeck from Lübeck is the one who, by his gentleness of soul and the power of his noble spirit, has gathered all the others around him and has inspired them to everything magnificent. He may be the greatest artist now living, and you would be astounded if you saw his work. Besides this, he is true humility and modesty personified. Pforr you know already through his works; he possesses the noblest and most faithful heart in the world, an imperturbable solidity in things that he considers genuine, but also a severity, which often becomes harsh and is very detrimental to him. A chest illness, which has confined him to his bed for the whole time I have been here, makes him milder and kinder, but may God shorten his time of trial and give him the happiness and confidence which his noble heart so much deserves. Vogel from Zürich is a man vigorously and richly endowed by nature. With open heart and spirit he seizes upon everything beautiful, good, and kind that nature has sown in the souls of men in order to unite them. He feels all relations between hearts as pure and humanly beautiful as I have ever seen. In addition he possesses an astonishing artistic talent. He paints most gloriously episodes from Swiss history. Wintergerst from Swabia possesses in addition to an open mind for everything good and beautiful, all those virtues which are not well regarded now and are therefore named the lesser ones, but which will be inscribed large in heaven; humility, fidelity, thankfulness, helpfulness to the point of submission, attachment, and love. He works in the style of Michelangelo and is extremely active and busy.

. . . On our way here we found a man in Lodi, called Hottinger, who also belonged to them, but who had changed for the worse and had left. They regretted this loss of a soul, as one justly should, because it is the greatest loss. I have been accepted in his place; their joy in this is so great and unfeigned that I count it among the happiest events of my life; thus the distance from the fatherland becomes more endurable. You too, my dear Mossler, will envy me, but I hope you, too, will some day belong to us; you already do in your opinions, your endeavors, and your unity with me. However, since our company is republican in nature, everyone must and shall win the heart of everyone else, since love is the bond. No one can recommend anyone else; each must do it in his own way; then, however, he belongs for life and death. At the moment I am doing drawings for the song of the Nibelungs. Today I received the news that Remmer in Berlin wants to publish them under the very favorable conditions which I suggested to him. Thus my stay in Italy is assured in a very pleasant manner. I am selling to him each plate, three by four, each page for 12 *Carolin*. This is adequate, isn't it? But for myself I am, of course, making things hard as you can believe. This way it will not fail in its purpose to sow a little seed for the best of our nation.

Farewell dear, best friend. Eternally yours, Cornelius.

Canova visits London

Between 1801 and 1803 the seventh Earl of Elgin, then British Ambassador to the Ottoman Empire, arranged for the removal of sculptures from Athens, notably from the Parthenon. When one shipment of these arrived in London (another was sunk *en route*), they revealed an unexpectedly fluent style to connoisseurs who had been accustomed to seeing Roman copies rather than Greek originals. Rome was thenceforward challenged by London as a centre for studying classical art.

Antonio Canova had derived his neo-classical style of sculpture from the antiquities of Rome; he was deeply impressed on his London visit. The formality of his appreciative letter to Lord Elgin has, incidentally, the carefully judged tone of a Papal *cavaliere* writing to a fellow nobleman. The Elgin Marbles were bought by the British government in 1816, and entered the British Museum collection.

(to the Earl of Elgin)[4] London, 12th November 1815.

Allow me, my Lord, to express to you the lively sentiments of pleasure which I feel, from having seen in London the inestimable antique marbles brought by your Lordship from Greece. I can never satisfy myself with viewing them again and again; and although my stay in this great metropolis must of necessity be extremely short, I am still anxious to dedicate every leisure moment to the contemplation of these celebrated relics of ancient art. I admire in them the truth of nature combined with the choice of beautiful forms: everything about them breathes animation, with a singular truth of expression, and with a degree of skill which is the more exquisite, as it is without the least affectation of the pomp of art, which is concealed with admirable address. The naked figures are real flesh, in its native beauty. I esteem myself happy in having been able to see these masterpieces with my own eyes; and I should be perfectly contented with having come to London on their account alone. I am persuaded therefore that all artists and amateurs must gratefully acknowledge their high obligations to your Lordship, for having brought these memorable and stupendous sculptures into your neighbourhood. For my part I give you most cordially a thousand thanks: and I have the honour to be, &c. &c. &c, Canova.

Feuerbach reassures his mother

By the middle of the century, Rome was still attracting artists. It was the example of the Renaissance which gave Anselm Feuerbach courage to pursue his art. It was, incidentally, a year after this letter was written that Nathaniel Hawthorne was in Rome collecting material for *The Marble Faun*, quoted at the beginning of this chapter.

(to his mother)[5] Rome, January 15th, 1857.

My dear good mother,

I can tell you with a happy heart that you can forget your anxieties on my account. Your spiritual strength is great enough to look beyond the present and to feel that in spite of my moods, worries and struggles, something will come out of it all which will make the struggles worthwhile.

In the evenings I am engrossed in Dante's *Vita Nuova*. I discern from it that hearts in the 13th century could also beat anxiously and that spiritual raptures and faint-hearted vacillations threatened to undermine the youthful poet, and that a man who was able to write a divine comedy first had to undergo a great many physical and spiritual difficulties.

When I recollect that I saw with my own eyes the youthful Dante and his Beatrice in a chapel of the S. Maria Novella in Florence, then two pictures stand out clearly in my mind which have remained with me throughout the years since then: the second encounter in the *Vita Nuova*, and Francesca in Dante's hell. These are background images that pass before my eyes in the evenings, distant but sure. You will understand that Rome becomes dearer to my heart by the hour, and that it will certainly become indispensable to me. My present circumstances are clear and definite: for the last three months I have been living in the greatest simplicity and my application has remained the same and will continue to do so, since I feel well in body and mind. My needs are minimal with no fear of going short. Thus things are progressing and there is no occasion for any retreating . . .

I underpaint the pictures in my room, then I draw the individual groups on paper and carry them to completion from life as in Raphael's studies. That is done at the studio of a friend whose progress is close to my heart. He learns from me and advances me the money for models until I have sold the paintings for a higher price. Once I have made the sketches, I shut myself up in my room and perfect them. Things can't be simpler or more practical than this. By being involved in many things, one keeps me fresh for the other.

During spring and summer my earnings go towards planning better creations and so on.

If my way of life gives you concern, banish these feelings. It is not worth speaking of in comparison with what is yet to be achieved.

Academies and schools

The Flandrin brothers change their minds

Hippolyte Flandrin and his brother arrived in Paris in 1829 with letters of introduction from Lyon and with the intention of joining the studio of Hersent. As his reputation was not what they had expected, they decided that they would rather study under Ingres. This letter to their father explains the reasons. Incidentally, Hippolyte Flandrin only later spelt his name correctly.

(to M. Flandrin)[6] Paris, 14 April 1829

My dear father,
A small change in our plans which we think of making causes me to write again so soon. You know that we were more or less decided to go to M. Hersent; I have changed my ideas a little, and not from capriciousness. Here are the reasons. First, in Paris M. Ingres is considered to have much greater ability than M. Hersent; besides his school is much better organised and quieter. He does not allow there the bad behaviour which elsewhere discourages a better young student from staying. So, Papa, you see that there are good reasons for going to M. Ingres, but I do not wish to do anything without your consent; for the choice of a master is a very important matter. I would ask you to explain our reasons to Aunt Martin and to the family, and to make them see that this is not by caprice.

If you could reply to us immediately, you would give us great pleasure. Meanwhile, we shall not be lazy. We shall deliver letters of introduction, pay visits etc.. There is only the letter from the general to M. Hersent which disturbs me; but it seems to me that we could avoid taking it, and write to the general that strong considerations have prevented us from going to M. Hersent. In any case we have several letters from him, and I feel that by using these others, we would not seem to be making little of his support.

We embrace you whole heartedly, also dear Maman and Caroline. We pray every day for our good sister. Waiting to hear from you, I am with respect and submission,

Your son, Hypolite.

The Rome Prize

The brothers made a good decision. Ingres encouraged and supported both of them, even remitting fees when he realised that they were in financial difficulties. The younger brother became a landscapist, and Hippolyte Flandrin after the success recorded in the following letter, became a leading religious mural painter.

(to M. and Mme. Flandrin) Paris, 25 September 1832

My dear father and mother,
I am writing for you to share our joy. I worked well, I gave myself a good deal of trouble, but I have been rewarded by my master's satisfaction; indeed, I shall tell you all about it.

Today, 25 September, our pictures are on exhibition. When the time of opening approached, I really had palpitations, for it is frightening to present one's work for the first time to the criticism, the censure of the public. At last the doors were opened. The public came in, and from behind I looked at the reactions of the groups of spectators. I first saw an enormous group round my picture, and then a large number of people whom I did not know asked me if I were not M. Flandrin? When I said yes, they complimented me. A moment later our fellow students arrived all at once. They looked, they judged, and then they came to me, shook my hand and pressed it, crowded round and embraced me. Oh! How these expressions of friendship gave me pleasure! Soon students from other ateliers arrived. Many of them added their congratulations to those of my fellow students, and their number had been increased again by a crowd of people I had never seen among whom were journalists, as you can see in the *Constitutionel* for the 26th. I was delighted with the general approval, but that of M. Ingres was missing; he had not yet seen my picture, and I was anxious. I went to see him at midday and I told him what had happened at the exhibition. He cried for joy, and told me to come back at five o'clock when he would have seen it.

Meanwhile I went back to the exhibition. All the time there was a crowd round my picture, and this lasted until the evening. Five o'clock came, I went to my master. He greeted me with open arms, embraced me, told me that few painters had made such a brilliant debut, that he was proud to have taught me, in fact a mass of flattering things. I repeat all this because you are my mother, my father, my brother and what pleases me will make you happy. And certainly, I could not receive a sweeter reward than M. Ingres' satisfaction and the way he expressed it. At all events the results of this day is that the artists and the public have decided by a great majority that I deserve the prize. With the public and M. Ingres, I really think I deserve the prize; but I do not believe I shall get it.

Today, Thursday 27, the crowd is as numerous as yesterday and they say the same thing. Many people have visited M. Ingres and congratulated him, which gives him acute pleasure. This morning he saw his students and much praised my picture to them. He spoke of us with such kindness and affection! It is certainly much more than I had expected.

Today, the 28th, there's still a crowd in front of my picture. Everyone assures me that I shall win, but I don't believe it, because the cabal is horribly active.

We have now arrived at Saturday 29. This is the day of the decision, and nevertheless I am much calmer than I was waiting for M. Ingres' judgement. Now, he and the public have awarded me the prize. That's why I am calm. I have done what I could; I hope to bear with injustice, because I have done my duty.

For painters our struggle is between good and evil. These two principles will never be reconciled. Also our enemies will gather all their forces together. M. Ingres left me to go to the decisive meeting and said to me, 'We are going to see how far men can push evil.'

Well, I was wrong. I have the prize! Soon I will tell you about it at greater length. Goodbye, your son who loves you, who loves you well!

At the Académie Julian

The Parisian system of art education pivoted on the *Ecole des Beaux Arts*; it was to this school that painters and sculptors aspired, and from it that French candidates like Hippolyte Flandrin, as we have seen, might achieve the particular distinction of a scholarship in Rome. A normal route to the school was through one of the preparatory *ateliers*, such as that run by Rodolphe Julian.

Foreigners also attended the Académie Julian; Marie Bashkirtseff came from Russia as one of his foreign students in the 1880s. She is well known to students of literature for her outspoken and poignant diary, first published in 1884, the year she died at the age of 23. The diary was, incidentally, one of the elderly Gladstone's favourite books, and was enthusiastically read by Paula Modersohn-Becker.

Marie Bashkirtseff saw her choices as dying young if the consumption from which she suffered overcame her, or striving to be a great artist; but the latter choice seemed to be obstructed by the French teaching system. This reasoned and passionate letter expresses her resentment at the barring of the *Ecole des Beaux Arts* to women.

(to Monsieur Julian)[7]

Dear Master,

So much has been said about the rights of women and so many intelligent and learned people have treated the subject with ridicule that one is almost ashamed to mention the subject; and yet the rights and the equality we claim have nothing to do with politics and have no connection whatever either with nihilism, or socialism, or Bonapartism, or the right to vote, or the eligibility of women to public office.

All these questions have been everywhere agitated; many instances of the injustice with which the weaker sex is treated have been brought forward; there is one, however, that has been mentioned by no one, perhaps because it is the most real, most striking and the most cruel of all – the absence of a School of Fine Arts for women.

How comes it, foreigners ask in wonder, that women are admitted to the School of Medicine, and that the School of Fine Arts is closed against them? At St. Petersburg, at Stockholm women are received at the Academy, and neither city pretends to be the equal of Paris!

Exactly, many say to us; and this is the best argument that can be used against you; in France, in Paris, such a thing would not be possible.

And why not, we ask?

To this they respond by a long discourse, under three heads, bristling with conclusions, all going to prove that our society is rotten and that the immorality of the French nation is such that what would be practicable elsewhere would not be at all practicable in France. And we retort by repeating, in the first place, that women are admitted to the School of Medicine – we will afterward specify the branches they are allowed to study – and that in the School of Fine Arts (as in the countries we have mentioned) they come in contact with the men pupils. The aesthetic course is pursued by both sexes together only in Sweden. And since in France women and men attend the various courses together, in what respect would these courses be more dangerous or more objectionable if pursued at the school. The studios in which they work with the model are separate.

The model in the men's class is nude; in that of the women he wears drawers like those worn by the bathers at Trouville and Dieppe, whom the most modest of ladies do not scruple to look at. So that, while the pupils are separated where it would be objectionable for them to study together, they are together where it would be to their advantage to be so.

Great publicity is given to the competition for admission and to the expulsions, which contributes not a little to the maintenance of order at the school.

The legend of the woman artist, of that vagabond and perverted being without industry or talent, – repulsive, hungry, beautiful, – who always comes to bad end, is a story in which little faith is placed now, although it has been the custom to cloak under the noble and honored name of *artist* a multitude of things which for the most part bear no relation to art. The old prejudice, however, has only been replaced by an excessively vague idea of what would be possible. The type is no longer grotesque, it no longer possesses any interest. It is not the few individuals who come under our notice, the charlatans, the young ladies who make copies at the Louvre or who have learned to paint pretty pictures in fashionable studios, who can enlighten us on this point. It is at the multitude, embracing a not inconsiderable number of talented pupils, who study art seriously in private studios – it is at this large number, who have really an amount of talent which would astonish those who ridicule the work of women, that we must look if we would know how interesting these workers are and by means of what incredible labors they succeed in acquiring a tolerably good education, faulty though it may be in many respects.

The studio of m. X – , which is the studio most numerously attended, contains more than fifty pupils.

Those who scoff at feminine talent can never know how many women who have taken up art seriously, women of genuine and remarkable talent, have been discouraged and their talents wasted through a vicious or incomplete education. The woman artist is quite as interesting as the man artist. It may be said that with two or three exceptions there has been no example of a woman having produced any work of art comparable to the best work of men artists. Yes, but the men receive, in one of the best schools in the world, an intelligent and comprehensive education; during the whole day they are surrounded by works of art, their eyes rest only on pure lines and brilliant colors, they breathe an atmosphere that opens their souls to inspiration and develops the wings of their imagination, on which they may soar to the heights of genius. And for women, nothing; or the chance of private studios.

What is there surprising, then, in the fact that with two or three exceptions there have never been women artists of real importance. And why this injustice toward woman, who has proved herself a thousand times more courageous, more persevering, obliged as she is to struggle not only against the poverty – unhappily common to both male and female artists – but also against terrible prejudices and difficulties without number, lacking even the freedom of movement which men have?

It is to man, who by his very nature has all the facilities for study, that all the means are given; and to woman, whom nature has deprived of freedom of movement and who has to struggle against everything, that this instruction is denied. There are too many women artists already, it may be said; woman was made for home. Alas, it is not by depriving them of the means of satisfying a noble passion that they will be inspired with a desire to spin wool. Why not afford women of ambition this glorious outlet? Why not encourage these aspirations towards the great, the beautiful, the useful, by making Paris the capital of the world, which like ancient Rome claims to be the *curia dignitatis gymnasium litterarum, domicilium verborum mundi, patriam libertatis?*

To accomplish this an appeal should be made to all artists. But these are not serious objections; and if they were the only ones nothing would be easier than to establish two studios of thirty or forty pupils each; there are facilities in plenty. But that would displease Messieurs the professors, in the first place, because it would be an innovation, a change, and routine is one of the flowers which thrives best in our institutes – and then, women! It is not worth thinking seriously about. Would it be possible for a woman to work seriously? Yes, she can work seriously, and there are even many who think she can, while saying to the contrary. But what would you have? It is so common to look down upon women. It is so common that it should cease to be practiced, and that it should be considered better taste not to do so.

It is to persons of enlightenment, to artists, to the disciples of art, who see only pure lines and brilliant colors, who breathe an atmosphere that opens the soul to the inspiration of what is puissant and beautiful, and develops the wings of the imagination on which they may soar to the heights of genius – it is to the friends of progress and of justice, that an appeal should be made.

France has a genius for painting.

When Julian sought to dissuade her from continuing in his *atelier*, on the grounds that 'she could do nothing more', Marie Bashkirtseff protested. The background to this letter is complicated, as there was some jealousy at work; Julian favoured another woman artist and promoted her work; indeed, dear reader, he married her.

(to M. Julian)

In order not to dispute with you *viva voce*, dear director, I write to you; otherwise it would be impossible for me to preserve the necessary calmness.

In my desire to find an explanation of the persistent discouragement you heap upon me with such delightful calmness, I form many conjectures. Perhaps I have lost my mind like the *Greco* or like Madame O'Connell, and am painting locomotives and cathedrals for human faces; in that case it would be necessary to take serious steps to prevent me from running about loose. Or perhaps you think that all the flatteries I receive have made me inordinately conceited, and that at all costs it is necessary to take down my pride.

Or perhaps –

But you know well that I do not believe at all, at all, in your candor; *you know* that I judge myself impartially, and that I am much more than discouraged; a discouragement to which you have contributed with a thirty-six horse power, but for which I bear you no ill will. Why do you keep up the farce of pretending to believe me blinded and crazed by vanity? Why do you torture me by maddening warnings? If it is to put me beside myself, you have succeeded; in future I shall try not to listen to your perfidious advice; that is all.

But if it is for my good, know that you deceive yourself, and most disastrously so for me. When one really desires to help people, when one really thinks they are in danger of drowning, one does not amuse one's self by filling their pockets with lead.

Besides, you do not believe a word of what you say when you talk about studies made at home or out of doors, which you make up into a bundle, perfidiously call pictures, and then use to crush me.

Have you, then, ever thrown in the faces of your X – 's, and other shining lights, their academic casts? My *pictures* are no worse than those, only I would at any time rather *fail* in a sincere and interesting study than succeed in a model, the more so as the knowledge acquired is the same in both; the process is only different.

That I have not reached my aim, that I am not a master, that I have still a great deal to learn, is evident; but between that and coming to tell me that I know not what terrible catastrophe has happened, that I can no longer do anything – that all is over – there is a great difference.

What I have produced is not much; but, after all, the pictures are there and they were not painted by the cook of the *Café Anglais* to amuse himself.

As a *result* they count for nothing; but they are studies as good as other studies; and then, since you keep such exact records, consult those records, and you will see that I have not even had the necessary time to pass through all the stages of decadence, through which the individuals you so often cite have passed. Deducting the time lost by illness, I have spent three years painting. This is an age for my impatience, but judging dispassionately, it is not long. So you see everything is opposed – the time I have spent in painting and my own inclination – to my accepting the role of retired pupil, which you wish to confer upon me.

The first of what you treacherously call my paintings was done in 1880, after eighteen months study, during twelve months only of which I worked all day. The last was done in the spring of 1882, during convalescence after an illness, when I had fever at least once a week. In the interval I exhibited the very mediocre 'Atelier' (without mention); and according to what even your most hostile young ladies say, I have rather improved than gone back since then. This brings me to that silly nonsense about exhibiting which you seem to regard as an impossibility. I should perhaps make as honorable an appearance as Miss K – , otherwise it would be necessary to return to the supposition that I am mad, *à la Greco.*

The more I think about it, the more I am convinced that you must have some inexplicable motive in seeking to crush me. You seem positively to delight in heaping discouragements of the most torturing kind upon me. It is plain that you do not consider what a terrible, I might almost say what a criminal thing it is to say to one who passionately longs to learn and study, 'You! You can do nothing more!' It is a moral assassination, more cruel than the assassination of the body, for you repeat it daily.

If you have any object in this, I cannot discover what it is. To affirm brutally that I can do nothing more is a very serious matter, and, in short – you know nothing about it. It will only result in a paralysis of the faculties and eight pages of literature. How will that profit you?

Now outside the art question, for which I hate you, for you have done me the greatest possible injury, we are good friends, and the proof is that on Sunday you dine at the Rue Ampère.

Herkomer and his school

Also in the 1880s, a school was established at Bushey in Hertfordshire by Hubert Herkomer, who aimed at encouraging painters in his vein of realism. A strength of the school was its friendly atmosphere, unlike the tough conditions found elsewhere. In Paris, for example, 'jokes could turn into brutal ragging; the most common procedure was to hang the victim upside down from the rungs of a ladder for several hours. Those living near the *Ecole des Beaux Arts* often rescued young men who had been abandoned in this position against a wall. It sometimes happened that these ordeals ended in broken limbs.'[8] Nor was bullying unknown in London; in a similar incident an envious fellow student maltreated the young Millais, who had won a medal at the Royal Academy Schools; the bully 'with the help of two other small boys whom he had compelled to remain, hung him downwards out of the window, tying his legs up to the iron of the window-guards with scarves and strings. There he hung over the street in a position which shortly made him unconscious, and the end might have been fatal had not some passers-by, seeing the position of the child rung the door-bell and secured his immediate release.'[9]

Bushey was, by comparison, a country idyll. Herkomer felt, after fifteen years, that he would like to use the prefix 'Royal' for his school. He was not successful in his request from which extracts are here given.

(from an official application)[10]

It is the first school of painting ever established away from and yet within easy reach of a large town. That in itself is of infinite advantage, artistically and morally – artistically because the students can go straight from painting in the life room to outdoor nature and landscapes; socially, because it means safe camaraderie between the sexes. Further the living is cheap. Yet the influence of the school means ten thousand pounds a year (at least) to the village . . .

The letter continues by describing the preliminary and life classes of the school, which was purely a school of painting.

All attempts at rowdyism, such as we see so much of in continental schools, subject the student to an immediate dismissal. That they respect my wishes is shown in the fact that no one need watch them. They are on their honour and they know this, and in the fifteen years I have had next to no trouble. I wish here to emphasise the fact that I have done all I can to stay the fashion of students going abroad to study – to give them an artistic freedom not easily if at all obtained in England but without the dangerous atmosphere that surrounds an English temperament when abroad . . .

I receive the students of the Life Class (past and present) on two evenings in the week, when they can ask me questions and get answers. This keeps me in touch with them as individuals. It is the best form of lecturing on art to students.

In these fifteen years some sixty-two independent studios have sprung up in Bushey, built and occupied by students who have graduated in the school. These students who are, as it were, setting up as young masters, still keep in touch with me and obtain criticisms and help on their pictures.

Teachers and influences

Bilders as a student

A young artist might become completely absorbed in acquiring an artist's point of view, or indeed the points of view of several artists. This could be rather overwhelming, as a letter from a young Dutchman to his father demonstrates. Gerard Bilders was a realist painter, a member of the Hague School. In the following letter he cites J. H. Weissenbruch as a landscapist, and Baron Gudin who was admired for the atmospheric effects of his marine paintings.

(to his father)[11]

Thus I always return to the old and eternal themes of pictures, nothing but pictures. I should like to know if for instance a carpenter is condemned to see in every tree, even a newly planted white willow – if the latter did not serve exclusively for wooden shoes – fine boards for a table, like we are doomed to see pictures in everything, to note colour or design or witty forms, even in the half-eaten roll we breakfast on. A pretty girl is always called a nice 'type'; of a sitting lady we always note the 'witty' pleats of her skirt; a bridge with a few old poles and a red-tiled house becomes a Weissenbruch; when we see a lean cow we think of Potter, and there isn't a thunderstorm without someone whispering almost inaudibly: Gudin! It is terrible to be so heavily bowed down under the tyranny of one's profession and when we go for a walk among colleagues we sometimes stipulate that no mention may be made of colours, drawings or paintings, but most times it is of little use because we have the added misfortune of being unable to talk about other subjects, owing to our lack of general knowledge. And we are not only a nuisance to ourselves and to each other, but to everybody else as well. I have even been troubling you again, for which I really ought to apologise.

An Oxford undergraduate

John Ruskin was hero-worshipped when he lectured at Oxford as the first Slade Professor, and, as this letter by a young undergraduate demonstrates, he gave considered critical attention to work shown to him. Selwyn Image was deeply influenced by Ruskin, whom he regarded all his life as his master.

(to his brother John Image)[12] 3 New Coll. St., Oxford

Febr. 8th, 1871

My dear John,

I am afraid you will long have been expecting to hear from me, after my promise of some ten days or more ago. It is only my old bad habit of putting things off till compelled into them by shame or necessity.

First of John Ruskin. I told you I was introduced last Saturday week: so at length my fondest dream has been just a little realized. I never met a man of such exquisitely kind, and courteous manner. The moment I got into the room he shook hands, and said 'I am very glad to see you, sir,' and offered me a chair. Naturally I felt dreadfully nervous, for I was in the presence of the man, in whom for the last year and a half I have conceived the clearest virtue and noblest wisdom to be, and from whose writings most certainly, (poorly as I have read them, and very poorly learnt their teachings), I have gained more of good than from any other man that ever lived. However by his wonderful gentleness he put me as much at my ease as possible; and asked to look at some drawings I had brought in my portfolio. I think he was fairly pleased with them, especially with an illuminated letter, which he said was 'beautifully drawn,' and 'the execution, what so few men got.' I go to the galleries and study with him, or for him (but he is generally there), an hour every day; and you can have no idea, how utterly feeble I find my work really is in everything except a mere rigid, agonized execution. It is I assure you sufficiently humiliating, and I get sometimes quite sick at heart about it: but some day far off I may perhaps learn to do a little good; and if I may only come to value what is true and noble in other's work I must rest content to let my own wretched feebleness lie in the dust. Indeed this is just what I feel, in other things as well as Art: it is no mere talk.

My friend was a great deal too pleased with the Illumination: he was very anxious for me to show it to Ruskin. I took it down to the Galleries, but could not muster courage enough at the last moment, knowing its real faultiness.

Ever yr most affectionate brother, Selwyn Image

Ruskin gives judgement

John Ruskin's practice as an art critic included practical help for those he wished to encourage. He is well known for having defended artists like Turner and the Pre-Raphaelites, as well as being notorious for having tried to put down Whistler. Relatively unknown artists particularly appreciated his support.

For example, he encouraged Frederic Shields whose designs for *The Plague of London* he saw in 1864. Ruskin wrote to him:

> I do not know any modern work which has impressed me
> with so much sense of a sterling, manly power of

> imaginative realisation as these Plague woodcuts of yours. They are quite magnificent. I shall feel it the merest and highest presumption to any power of guiding and advising you. A designer of your calibre *can* only do what he ought, and *he* only knows what he ought.

Nevertheless meekness was not Ruskin's outstanding characteristic, and he was not sure of Shields' abilities as a colourist. Ruskin's mind was put at rest a little later, as the evidence of Shields himself demonstrates. 'Mr Ruskin sent a fresh herring in water-colour by William Hunt, of exquisite colour; and I had the reward, when I took it and my copy to him at Denmark Hill, of hearing him say, "Well, if you had brought back your copy and retained the Hunt, I should never have known the difference." This settled the question of my eye for colour, hitherto in doubt.'[13]

Vernet praises a new method

Horace Vernet's most impressive work was the series of battle pictures commissioned by Louis Philippe for the Palace of Versailles. His high regard for the teaching of Lecoq de Boisbaudran is expressed in the following letter written to encourage the publication of a second edition of *The Training of the Memory in Art.*

Lecoq de Boisbaudran held that the aim of all teaching was 'to keep the artist's individual feeling pure and unspoiled, to cultivate it, and bring it to perfection.' He deprecated the copy books of classical figures commonly in use; 'for instance, I am perfectly aware of the strong objection that is felt against all copies, either drawn or engraved, especially those that represent figures or parts of figures. We are still suffering from the perfectly legitimate irritation caused by the dreadful copies of Reverdin and Julien, so full of complicated and pretentious cross-hatching.'

(to Lecoq de Boisbaudran)[14] Château de Champagnette
this 24th of September 1860

Dear Sir,

It is with great pleasure that I learn on my return from a tour in Britanny, that you intend to publish a second edition of your book

Memory in Art. I cannot wait till I get to Paris to beg you to push forward your enterprise, which deserves every encouragement. To formulate in writing the principles which you have employed with such success in your classes, is the surest way of making your method more widely known. It is a method completely new, for its purpose is to cultivate the power of retaining in the memory, what is fugitive in nature, such as expression, rapid movement, passing effects etc, things which it is quite hopeless to attempt to get from a model in the studio. Memory then is clearly of the greatest service.

The 'Institut' has already shown by its appreciation of what you have done how valuable it considers the education you are giving your pupils in this direction.

Personally I have the best reasons for being one of your most enthusiastic supporters, for I have made use of my memory all through my artistic career. I pledge you, therefore, to continue to make your ideas better known, for they are on the road to true progress, and open up new and far-reaching prospects in the teaching of art.

- Believe me, yours affectionately, Horace Vernet

Du Maurier feels bourgeois

George Du Maurier studied in Paris with the hope that he could become a painter. We are lucky in having a brilliant account of the atmosphere he knew there in his novel *Trilby*. He continued to work at improving his art in England; according to the evidence here, he was rather daunted by the unusual early success of Frederick Walker, who was admired by Ruskin.

Du Maurier's dashing and cosmopolitan letters exhibit a meld of English and French. This one has more than a glint of satire in its description of a latter-day Pre-Raphaelite evening party. By 1864 Du Maurier had been unnerved by the loss of the sight of one eye, but he had recently married and the couple's first child had just been born. He never returned to painting because he was offered a staff position on *Punch*; he was the successor to John Leech. Du Maurier proved to have a considerable talent for social satire. Indeed, his sharp observation of Jones (Burne-Jones was a later development for the painter's name) and his Pre-Raphaelite friends soon found its way into his *Punch* drawings.

(to his mother)[15] Saturday April, 1864

I have been getting through a good deal of work and am told that I improve. I don't improve fast enough to please myself though. I want very much to paint in watercolours, and hope to do something in Clovelly. I suppose you have read everywhere about little Fred Walker's unparalleled success; seven, eight hundred pounds offered for little watercolours, a couple of feet square, and more orders than he can paint. If he doesn't get spoilt, what a grand little fellow he must be; only 25! and such a nice lad, so modest. Whistler is getting on very well now, wonderfully so considering that he is the great genius and innovator, the sort of fellow that dies in a hospital, while centuries after he has a statue put up. The other night I went to a bachelor's party to meet Rossetti and Swinburne at Simeon Solomon's. Such a strange evening; Rossetti is the head of the pre-raphaelites, for Millais and Hunt have seceded; spoilt so to speak by their immense popularity; whereas Rossetti never exhibits and is comparatively unknown; this strange contempt for fame is rather grand. He is also a great poet, and his translations from the early Italian poets are the finest things in their way that have been done. As for Swinburne, he is without exception the most extraordinary man not that I have met only, but that I ever read or heard of; for three hours he spouted his poetry to us, and it was of a power, beauty and originality unequalled. Everything after seems tame, but the little beast will never I think be acknowledged for he has an utterly perverted moral sense, and ranks Lucrezia Borgia with Jesus Christ; indeed says she's far greater, and very little of his poetry is fit for publication. If you like I will copy one of his very mildest which has been published, namely Faustine, and send it you. These strange creatures all hang in a clique together, and despise everything but themselves; and really I don't wonder. Swinburne's French poetry is almost as fine as his English. The other day at Jones's he was asked to write verses for four pictures of the seasons Jones had just painted, and in *twenty minutes* he had produced four beautiful little latin poems!

Tom and I felt like two such bourgeois that night, so healthy and human; didn't get home till three, and wasn't it jolly just after this strange but gorgeous nightmare of an evening, to wake up and find a healthy innocent little baby weighing over twenty pounds.

Ce qui n'empêche pas that genius of this magnitude is a very divine and extraordinary gift, to be bowed down to and worshipped.

Pissarro helps his son

Students and artists needing to make their way in the world, then as now, often relied on parental help, which Camille Pissarro was prepared to give. Pissarro had an intimate understanding of his son's difficulties from the struggles he and his fellow Impressionists had overcome. Lucien Pissarro in due time established his English career, partly through admirable illustrated books published at the Eragny Press which he founded in 1896.

(to Lucien Pissarro)[16] Paris, September 5, 188[?]6

My dear Lucien,

Your mother insists that I should not give you 300 francs per month. For a long time now she has been arguing about this with me. I try to reconcile all parties but I don't succeed very well. All I can tell you at the moment is that you can be sure I will help you if conditions are not too bad.

I am writing you hastily, your mother may come to Paris today. I shall not discuss the question of money with her, it would accomplish absolutely nothing and advance us not a step. She doesn't realize the difficulties of a beginner in art, nor does she understand that one can find a place in this field if one has the will to do so. And I have listened and shall continue to listen only to what my experience counsels. You have to get in a good position to succeed in your field and, as you say, we have to prevent the other[s ?] profit from what you have taken so many pains to establish. So, for my part, I will do my utmost to send you the 300 francs without speaking about it. I insist on this, it is to avoid wearisome discussions with your mother. I will send you the money some other way, this will depend on the circumstance, but in any case I shall send it. I am forewarning you, that is all. It is disagreeable to be underhanded, but, damn it, it's no go otherwise! – This is the only way to avoid arguments!

Your mother is afraid that I am helping you too much and thus depriving your brothers, but this is not so; when their turn comes, I expect you to be more secure and I will do for them what I am doing for you three; it's not much, but I do the best I can.

If things don't improve we'll have to get along somehow. . . . Durand-Ruel fears there will be a terrific crash in this blessed America: this matter oinage of money. If the president elected is in favor of this, we shall have our hands full.

The American Impressionist

Mary Cassatt faced a different set of difficulties. Her family was well-to-do; for example, her brother Alexander was the sort of railway magnate who arrived in England to be accorded a special tug to take him off the Liverpool boat, and a private carriage for his train journey to London. In her social milieu, Mary Cassatt's wish to be a professional artist was eccentric. Her first studies were in Philadelphia, but she considered them inadequate, so Europe was her artistic salvation. Here is an extract from a letter about a sketching trip, on her first visit, which lasted from 1866 to the beginning of the Franco-Prussian war.

(to Lois Cassatt)[17] August 1, 1869

The Savoyards are a most civil people and talk a sort of mixture of French and Italian very hard to understand. We are just on the borders of Italy, we took a mountain exursion the other day and waded up to our ankles in snow, but were rewarded by a magnificent view of Mont Blanc and the St Bernard, however we think we will rest satisfied with that and not try it again as we had to walk some twelve hours.

In the 1870s she studied in Italy, Spain and the Low Countries, besides studying with conventional teachers in Paris; but she found she was more impressed by the strength of the art of Courbet and Degas. It was Degas who invited her in 1877 to join the Impressionist group, and he became her close friend (all of his letters to her, by the way, she burnt). The seeds were sown for the flowering of her intimate art, most especially the studies of mothers and children from the 1880s onwards.

2
The Practice of Art

Those letters by artists in which they describe their aims are among the most fascinating and instructive of all. It is best when the artist has a correspondent whose sympathy is assured and who knows something of the difficulties of artistic achievement. Vincent van Gogh, for example, was fortunate in being able to share his intimate thoughts and ideals with his brother Theo; John Constable had the unfailing friendship of John Fisher. Such letters are those most often quoted in monographs, catalogues and histories, and hence this chapter has only a token showing of them. After all, does not every anthologist hope at best to inspire or at worst to provoke the reader to explore further?

Another source for discovering more about artists' intentions is less private writing, some of which in the nineteenth century was cast in epistolary form. It was a time when letters, lectures and sermons could all find themselves transmuted into books and some celebrities even found difficulty in distinguishing which sort of audience they were addressing. Disraeli knew and judged his audiences well, but Queen Victoria famously complained about Gladstone that he talked to her as if she were a public meeting.

In England Ruskin was a prolific writer of private and public letters, and a publisher of lectures; here is an extract from his third letter to beginners in *The Elements of Drawing* (1857).

> My dear reader, – If you have been obedient, and have hitherto done all that I have told you, I trust it has not

> been without much subdued remonstrance, and some serious vexation. For I should be very sorry if, when you were led by the course of your study to observe closely such things as are beautiful in colour, you had not longed to paint them, and felt considerable difficulty in complying with your restriction to the use of black, or blue, or grey. You *ought* to love colour, and to think nothing quite beautiful or perfect without it; and if you really do love it, for its own sake, and are not merely desirous to colour because you think painting a finer thing than drawing, there is some chance you may colour well . . . Every hue throughout your work is altered by every touch that you add in other places; so that what was warm a minute ago, becomes cold when you have put a hotter colour in another place, and what was in harmony when you left it, becomes discordant as you set other colours beside it; so that every touch must be laid, not with a view to its effect at the time, but with a view to its effect in futurity, the result upon it of all that is afterwards to be done being previously considered. You may easily understand that, this being so, nothing but the devotion of life, and great genius besides, can make a colourist.[1]

For Ruskin, the best drawing-masters were the woods and the hills. In Germany this view had already been expressed on *Nine Letters of Landscape Painting* (1831) by Carl Carus in a mystic's approach to nature. His second letter starts as follows.

> Let us go now, dear friend! go to a closer discussion of the purpose and the meaning of landscape painting: an art which belongs to the recent times and which in general is much less enclosed in itself, and perhaps still looking forward to its Golden Age, than the other arts, most of which resemble the head of Janus, looking backward, or even stand as memorials to better days on the graves of the past. Any imitative art has necessarily a twofold effect on us: once through the nature of the copied object, whose particular property affects us in a way similar to nature itself; and next as a work of art which is a creation of man's

> intellect, and through a true experience lifts the kindred spirit above the commonplace (in the same way that the world in the highest sense may be called an appearance of divine thought).[2]

In a theoretical vein, a private letter from Philip Otto Runge ventures into aesthetics; when the artist wrote in 1802, he was on his way to formulating a wider theory of art, some of it published in 1810. Here is the extract from Runge's letter.

> Thus art is the most beautiful endeavour, if it begins with that which belongs to all and is in unison with it. Therefore I will once again mention here now the requirements for a work of art follow each other, not only with regard to essential importance, but also with regard to the way in which they should be formed:
>
> 1. Our awareness of God,
> 2. The perception of ourselves in relationship with the whole, and out of these two:
> 3. Religion Art; that is, to express our highest feelings in words, tones, or pictures; and there the plastic art looks first for:
> 4. the object; then
> 5. the composition,
> 6. the design,
> 7. the colour-scheme,
> 8. balance,
> 9. the colour-scale,
> 10. the tone.
>
> In my opinion no work of art can be formed by any means, if the artist does not start from the first motives. Also, in no other way is a work of art eternal: for the eternity of a work of art certainly is only in its relationship to the soul of the artist, and by this, it is a picture of the eternal origin of his soul . . .[3]

Letters written privately did not often take up such issues of theory in the arts. In the following choice of letters about ideas and practice, most of the writers are struggling with less abstruse problems.

Artistic ideas

Rethel's stages in picture-making

Alfred Rethel is best known as an engraver. Burne-Jones was a firm admirer; 'By absolutely perfect wood-engraving, I mean such work as all the sixteenth-century engravings and such as those quite perfect examples in Rethel's "Dance of Death" and the "Friend and Avenger". I don't believe that any attempt to express more than they do could possibly be successful.'[4] In this letter Rethel discusses his working methods as a painter.

(to his brother)[5] Monday evening, Frankfurt.

Dear Otto,

As far as my creative activities are concerned, since your last visit and particularly during last winter, I can truly say that I have made some progress. I am now being very strict with myself as regards not so much the finished execution of detail, as in the preserving and conveying of the original impulse in my paintings. E.g. I work over the head 3–4 times as it appears to me clearly and distinctly at the time. This is not a formal over-painting, but rather an enlivening process of sketching, often with only a few strokes, thus leading back to my first experience. . . .

There are stages that have to be gone through in the execution of a picture. In the case of sketches, cartoons, colour-sketches and the under-painting of a picture, a freshness of spirit and a novelty of subject help considerably in bringing the work quickly to a certain point. As a rule, when over-painting, these two aids are lacking, and when one realises how far removed the work is from the original impulse, then a painful state of irresolution and experimentation intrudes, and only a mental effort and a certain sense of duty helps one to pass through this stage. It is now that the third phase occurs; often it is the most distressing one imaginable, and it is certainly the most important. The work has reached a certain level of completion both in composition and colour; it is then that one asks oneself anxiously; but does it conform to my original idea? Is this picture with its scumbles and glazes the one I wanted to paint?

In giving their verdicts, the unengaged always comment on nonessentials of the painting, but one can clearly tell that the impression of the whole has not affected them; rather it has left them cold. Oh these are the moments of extreme sadness when one feels that the artistic spark of the painting is almost extinguished, that it has turned simply into an insipid arithemetical problem.

But one does not know how or where to remedy the evil. The sad moment of flatness and stupidity arrives. One feels stupefied. At such times one should be sufficiently master of oneself to set aside the palette, not to attempt anything, but to turn the picture to the wall, leaving it there for a considerable length of time, even though other work is being undertaken, one's mind subconsciously dwells with the misbegotten child and gradually, quite without intention and quite naturally, one reconciles it to the original idea. Gradually one makes peace with the picture which now lives in the memory; one does not find it quite so objectionable, one is possessed by a burning desire to finish it; one comes along, turns the painting round, puts it up on the easel and – one is transported rather ungently from heaven to reality.

The picture is still the same. But one looks at it with quite different eyes; like lightning the true artistic spirit enters, checking, assessing, accompanied by a warm glow and a refreshed imagination that recognises what is lacking. It takes hold of the palette and every brush stroke fits. It is true that in the process here and there the delicate but calculated execution suffers as a result of fiery intensity, but that is no loss when one weighs it against the gains which gladden the heart. One wants to advance and improve everything at once, and thus one enters the fourth phase, wonderful and rewarding, leading to the finale. Once more may we take pleasure in our day's work, being once again aware of what we want. Then we may confidently allow the reins to slacken a little; we make blunders as a result and allow gross carelessness – the German character vouches for that – but this will not be the main defect; rather it will be a too painstaking execution of detail.

Constable considers the sky

John Constable was one of the outstanding letter writers among nineteenth century artists. His correspondence to his family and friends gives an extensive view of his personal and professional life.

One of Constable's closest friends was John Fisher, Archdeacon of Salisbury, to whom he wrote the following letter about landscape, and in particular the importance of the sky. The text is here taken from the *Memoirs* published by Constable's colleague, the American painter C. R. Leslie. We now know that it is not quite what Constable wrote; Leslie tidied up Constable's prose, not always to advantage. An example of Constable's writing *verbatim* is to be found in the next chapter, in a letter to his wife.

(to John Fisher)[6] Hampstead, October 23rd, 1821.

My dear Fisher, . . . I am most anxious to get into my London painting-room, for I do not consider myself at work unless I am before a six-foot canvas. I have done a good deal of skying, for I am determined to conquer all difficulties, and that among the rest. And now talking of skies, it is amusing to us to see how admirably you fight my battles; you certainly take the best possible ground for getting your old friend out of a scrape (the example of the old masters). That landscape painter who does not make his skies a very material part of his composition neglects to avail himself of one of his greatest aids. Sir Joshua Reynolds, speaking of the landscape of Titian, of Salvator, and of Claude, says: 'Even their *skies* seem to sympathise with their subjects.' I have often been advised to consider my sky as *'a white sheet thrown behind the objects'*. Certainly, if the sky is obtrusive, as mine are, it is bad; but if it is evaded, as mine are not, it is worse; it must and always shall with me make an effectual part of the composition. It will be difficult to name a class of landscape in which the sky is not the key-note, the standard of scale, and the chief organ of sentiment. You may conceive, then, what a 'white sheet' would do for me, impressed as I am with these notions, and they cannot be erroneous. The sky is the source of light in nature, and governs everything; even our common observations on the weather of every day are altogether suggested by it. The difficulty of skies in painting is very great, both as to composition and execution; because with all their brilliancy, they ought not to come forward, or, indeed, be hardly thought of any more than extreme distances are; but this does not apply to phenomena or accidental effects of sky, because they always attract particularly. I may say all this to you, though *you* do not want to be told that I know very well what I am about, and that my skies have not been neglected, though they have often failed in execution, no doubt, from an over-anxiety about them, which will alone destroy that easy appearance which nature always has in all her movements.

How much I wish I had been with you on your fishing excursion in the New Forest! What river can it be? But the sound of water escaping from mill-dams, etc., willows, old rotten planks, slimy posts, and brickwork, I love such things. Shakespeare could make everything poetical; he tells us of poor Tom's haunts among 'sheep cotes and mills'. As long as I do paint, I shall never cease to paint such places. They have always been my delight, and I should indeed have been delighted in seeing what you describe, and in your company, 'in the company of a man to whom nature does not spread her volume in vain'. Still I should paint my own places best; painting is with me but another word for feeling, and I associate 'my careless boyhood' with all that lies on the banks of the Stour; those scenes made me a painter, and I am grateful; that is, I had often thought of pictures of them before I ever touched a pencil, and your picture is the strongest instance of it I can recollect; but I will say no more, for I am a great egotist in whatever relates to painting. Does not the Cathedral look beautiful among the golden foliage? its solitary grey must sparkle in it.

Sisley is averse to theory

Alfred Sisley was not keen to answer a question about what his aesthetic might be; nevertheless, he was prepared to give some valuable insight into his own aims, such as enveloping objects in light, and like Constable, paying especial attention to the sky.

This letter is not dated, though probably written around 1880.

(to an unknown correspondent)[7]

It is a ticklish thing to put down on paper what an artist calls his 'aesthetic'.

The aversion to theory that Turner felt, I feel too, and I believe it's much easier to talk about masterpieces than to create them, whether with the brush or in any other way.

As you know, the charm of a painting is many-sided. The subject, the motif, must be set down in a simple way, easily understood and grasped by the beholder. By the elimination of superfluous detail, the spectator should be led along the road that the artist indicates to him, and from the first be made to notice what the artist has felt.

Every picture shows a spot with which the artist has fallen in love. It is this, amongst other things, which gives the work of Corot and Jongkind its unsurpassed charm.

The animation of the canvas is one of the hardest problems of painting. To give life to the work of art is certainly one of the most necessary tasks of the true artist. Everything must serve this end: form, colour, surface. The artist's impression is the life-giving factor, and only this impression can free that of the spectator.

And, though the artist must remain master of his craft, the surface, at times raised to the highest pitch of liveliness, should transmit to the beholder the sensation which possessed the artist.

You see that I am in favour of a variation of surface within the same picture. This does not correspond with customary opinion, but I believe it to be correct, particularly when it is a question of rendering a light effect. Because when the sun lets certain parts of a landscape appear soft, it lifts others into sharp relief. These effects of light, which have an almost material expression in nature, must be rendered in material fashion on the canvas.

Objects must be portrayed in their particular context, and they must, especially, be bathed in light, as is the case in nature. The progress to be achieved in the future will consist in this. The means will be the sky (the sky can never be merely a background). Not only does it give the picture depth through its successive planes (for the sky, like the ground, has planes) but through its form, and through its relations with the whole effect, or with the composition of the picture, it gives movement . . .

I emphasise this part of a landscape because I would like you to understand the importance I attach to it.

An indication of this: I always begin a picture with the sky.

Seurat corrects his printers

The abstract theorising of Georges Seurat was very much in contrast with Sisley's more pragmatic approach to art. Seurat was a painter who was firmly possessive about his divisionist method, and anxious that he received all due credit for its innovatory character. It is not much of a surprise to find him writing in a letter to correct a printed text, going on to elucidate his more general theories.

(to Maurice Beaubourg)[8] August 28, 1890

In closing I will give you the note on esthetic and technique which finishes the study of my work by Monsieur Christophe, and which is my own. I have modified it somewhat, it not having been well understood by the printers.

Esthetic
Art is harmony.
Harmony is the analogy of opposites, the analogy of similar elements, of *value, hue,* and *line,* considered according to their dominants, and under the influence of lighting, in gay, calm, or sad combinations.
The opposites are:
For value, a more (luminous) for a darker one.
(light)
For hue, the complementaries, i.e., a certain red opposed to its complementary, etc.
(red-green
(orange-blue
(yellow-violet
For line, those forming a right angle.
Gaiety of value is the light dominant; of *hue,* the warm dominant; of *line,* lines above the horizontal.
Calmness of value is the equality of dark and light; of hue, of warm and cool; and the horizontal for line.
Sadness of value is the dark dominant; of hue, the cool dominant; and of line, downward directions.

Technique
Granting the phenomena of the duration of the light-impression on the retina, synthesis necessarily follows as a resultant. The means of expression is the optical mixture of values, of hues (of the local color and the color of the illuminating light; sun, oil, lamp, gas, etc., that is to say, of the lights and their reactions (shadows), in accordance with the laws of *contrast,* gradation and irradiation.
The frame is in a harmony opposed to that of the values, hues, and lines of the picture.

Van Gogh discusses colour with a colleague

Did Vincent van Gogh write the most famous artist's letters of the century? He was a painter who was passionate about directly conveying his ideas and feelings, and in his later work dared to make bold experiments. He had been inspired by the colour innovations of his Impressionist friends, and had used the divisionist technique promoted by Seurat; but he was searching for a greater intensity and was not satisfied. Here he expresses his sense of unease to his fellow artist Emile Bernard.

(to Emile Bernard)[9] Arles. Mid-June 1888

Dear old Bernard,

More and more it seems to me that the pictures which must be made so that painting should be wholly itself, and should raise itself to a height equivalent to the serene summits which the Greek sculptors, the German musicians, the writers of French novels reached, are beyond the power of an isolated individual; so they will probably be created by groups of men combining to execute an idea held in common.

One person may have a superb orchestration of colors and lack ideas. Another one is cram-full of new concepts, tragically sad or charming, but does not know how to express them in a sufficiently sonorous manner because of the timidity of a limited palette. All the more reason to regret the lack of co-operative spirit among the artists, who criticise and persecute each other, fortunately without succeeding in annihilating each other. You will say that this whole line of reasoning is banal – so be it! However, the thing itself – the existence of a renaissance – this fact is certainly no banality.

A technical question. Just give me your opinion of it in your next letter. I am going to put the *black* and the *white* on my palette and use them just as they are. When – and observe that I am speaking of the simplifications of color in the Japanese manner – when in a green park with pink paths, I see a gentleman dressed in black and a justice of the peace by trade (the Arab Jew in Daudet's 'Tartarin' calls this honorable functionary a *zouage de paix*), who is reading *l'Intransigeant* . . . Over him and the park sky of simple cobalt.

. . . Then why not paint the said *zouage de paix* with ordinary bone black and the *l'Intransigeant* with simple, quite raw white. For the

Japanese artist ignores reflected colors, and puts the flat tones side by side, with characteristic lines marking off the movements and the forms.

In another category of ideas – when for instance one composes a motif of colors representing a yellow evening sky, then the fierce hard white of a white wall against the sky may be expressed if necessary – and in this strange way – by raw white, softened by a neutral tone, for the sky itself colors it with a delicate lilac hue. Furthermore, imagine in the landscape which is so naive, and a good thing, too, a cottage, whitewashed all over (including the roof). Standing in an orange field – certainly orange, for the southern sun and the blue Mediterranean provoke an orange tint that gets more intense as the scale of blue colors gets a more vigorous tone – then the black note of the door, the windows and the little cross on the ridge of the roof produce a simultaneous contrast of black and white just as pleasing to the eye as that of blue and orange.

Or, to take a more amusing motif: imagine a woman in a black and white checked dress in the same primitive landscape with a blue sky and orange soil – that would be a rather funny sight, I think. In Arles they often do wear black and white checks.

Suffice to say that black and white are also colors, for in many cases they can be looked on as colors, for their simultaneous contrast is as striking as that of green and red, for instance.

The Japanese make use of it for that matter. They express the mat and pale complexion of a young girl and the piquant contrast of the black hair marvellously well by means of white paper and four strokes of the pen. Not to mention their black thornbushes starred all over with a thousand white flowers. . . .

Repin appreciates sympathy from Tolstoy

Tolstoy's great novels, *War and Peace* and *Anna Karenina* were less important to him in his later years than concern for simple and deep truths, found, as he believed in fables, the Bible and the faith of ordinary people. This attitude to life was a bond with Ilya Repin who had similar beliefs and interests, which were expressed in his stirring realist pictures. Their common interests resulted in a correspondence between the two men.

The two pictures mentioned by Repin are 'Seeing off the Recruit' (about which Tolstoy appears to have been critical), and a famous picture showing the Cossacks of Zaporozhtsy writing a letter to the Turkish Sultan.

(to L. N. Tolstoy)[10] November 19, 1880
Moscow

How happy I am to receive your letters, Lev Nikolaevitch! I should confess to you, that I was very afraid after having written you a letter. I was very angry with myself and didn't expect you to answer . . . Oh, how glad and happy I am! Perhaps, you will visit again my shabby studio. Your remarks on my 'Seeing off' were precise. When I was finishing the picture, I began to feel that it looked rather cool and couldn't decide what to do. I lost all my interest in it and finished it because I had to finish it somehow.

You can't even imagine how worried I am with my lack of character, haste, and useless wishes. I can't find the bright idea that could be clearly expressed in plastic images . . .

For instance, now I am passionately working on 'Zaporozhtsy' for more than three weeks, but sometimes I have a feeling that the plot is bleak and doesn't deserve serious attention. I have done the half of it. Of course, it is a study, not a picture. You are absolutely right. That sounds strange, but at the very moment when I decided to give it up, I almost automatically picked up my palette and found myself working . . .

I want now to take something from the modern, most burning life. I even had an idea to change my address for Petersburg. I am getting tired of Moscow with its bourgeois atmosphere.

Excuse me for telling you my passing thoughts taking them from the top of my head.

Thank you again for your letters, they cheer me up. Please don't spare me, I love any remarks, and especially yours for their deep truth and bright intellect.

I should say that the photo of my picture is fairly bad, nevertheless, it doesn't alter the picture's composition.

Yours gratefully I Repin

Zorn argues for quality

Large pictures for exhibitions during the century reflected artists' ambitions both for recognition and hopes of official purchases. This was especially true in such countries as France where there was a system of purchasing for the State. In Sweden, too, some artists worked on a considerable scale, regarding this as a matter of prestige.

The following letter is a reply from Anders Zorn, who was working abroad at the time, to his fiancée.

(to Emma Lamm)[11] London 1885

I am happy that you do not judge my pictures by size as much as quality. But tell me wherein this greatness lies concealed? Perhaps you mean beauty? In that case I understand more easily and shall be more willing to strive to attain it. Beauty is great but there are many other things besides. If you believe that in our times one can infuse beauty into eyes, nose and mouth just as in a big composition containing hundreds of people then I can still hope, even though it seems I have been a failure so far. The other day I saw something great but not beautiful.

I was invited to visit an older artist – I entered a large and splendid studio and immediately my eyes fell upon a picture, an historical picture (Lady Hamilton, Lord Nelson etc.) a really grand work but, preserve me, anything but beautiful. I could not and did not want to say anything.

The artist informed me that he was not interested in everyday life, only the great historical scenes – just as I was ready to leave he happened to produce a study. It was only some mummies from the museum that he had painted, but such colour and feeling as were contained in that canvas I have rarely seen before. This was in fact a good illustration of what I have written above. I hope you would not like me to mistake my calling as he has done.

Material considerations

As well as with theories and ideas in art, artists needed to deal with practical matters. Sculptors had to make choices of materials, for example clay, bronze, or stone including marble; and they needed to establish how to carry out commissions. Painters took advantage of the results of advances in chemistry which made new pigments available, and the convenience of metal tubes as paint containers instead of pigs' bladders. Some instructive and interesting letters on such topics were written by a number of artists.

Schadow is kept busy in Berlin

Gottfried Schadow was a prominent and successful sculptor in Berlin, with an active professional practice. We are lucky to have this letter from him, rather formal in tone, describing his practice in some detail. The first paragraph with its disclaimer about artists' letters finds many echoes through the centuries.

(to Bottiger)[12] Berlin, 15 September 1802

For some time it has been in my mind, my honoured friend, to send you news of myself, and, as it were, to render you an account of my life as an artist. But writing calls for a special mood, and that visits us but seldom; the inclination, I would say, never at all; we artists have no inclination save for our own work; and if we are to write at all, we shall do better to wait until our thoughts are gathered into a flood that must burst out to relieve our hearts. You wish it, so I will tell you about myself.

The great part of my time is occupied with commissioned work, I seldom have an hour to give to my own whims; yet so many ideas come to mind which one would at least wish to capture with pencil on paper, and others to which one would like to give complete form!

I sometimes think of myself as a worthy craftsman, plying his trade in the town by carrying out his customers' orders. He has his workshop, his assistants and apprentices, and he will provide you with anything that falls within his own line of business. For neither I, my assistants nor my boys are clock-watchers, it is simply a love of the work that brings us to it.

No; the only actual craftsmen among us are the stone-mason, the engraver, the polisher and the moulder; but the moulder has two different parts to play. He began life as a mason, then bettered himself by becoming a stucco-worker and after that, a man who wields hammer and chisel in obedience to strict mathematical precepts. He sets his plaster cast and his block of marble side by side, with a horizontal frame slung above the plumb-lines dangling over each of them at set distances; he measures the projections on the cast with a stick and cuts away the marble at the corresponding places, until his measuring rod goes as far in from the plumb-line on the marble as from the corresponding one on the plaster model. We call this 'fixing points', or rather 'pointing a figure'. The distances between the points are marked by circles, so that the block of marble is scattered all over with little pencil dots, like the sky with stars, and not one of them must be further to left or right, or higher or lower, than it actually is. This work calls for unwavering concentration and a genuine love of precision. For sculpture on a flat background – in low or high relief – the procedure is different, and makes use of what is called a 'crutch'; but I will say nothing of that, for mere description of such things cannot enable them to be visualised.

I have seldom been successful in conveying the idea of modelling and casting to a person who knows nothing of them; but even for the sake of the few one must make some attempt and it is worth while.

It may not add to the enjoyment of looking at a work of art, to know how it came into existence; but the artist's countrymen would surely hold him in affection and respect if they knew of the varied and irksome difficulties with which his mind and body must contend before a great work is brought to completion.

True, clay offers a soft pliable mass, lending itself to the removal or addition of pieces; but several years' practice is required before one can build standing figures and deal successfully with unsupported portions. Arms, hands, fingers and any other comparatively thin portions dry more quickly than the rest, and need either outward props or inner framework of iron to keep them from collapsing. The clay model, once completed, is used to make a plaster cast, and the work thus changes from one material into another! Some people will ask 'why'? The answer is that clay shrinks and becomes appreciably smaller, and that in a dry and unfired condition it is extremely brittle. A dry clay model could not be moved round very much, and would soon break when large calipers were used on it for measuring purposes; it might be fired, but if it is of any great size there will be no kiln to take it; it should be hollowed out and may shatter into a myriad pieces under the action of heat. For safety's sake, therefore, the transformation into plaster is adopted, though admittedly expensive. . . .

Before preparing the final model, one makes a smaller one, to preserve one's idea; often, of course, a sketch is needed as well, being easier to show people or to send by letter; but it will not be much use to the sculptor, since it only shows *one* side, *one* aspect of the work.

If the statue is to be a clothed one, the clothes must first be arranged on a life-sized lay figure. Some garments may have to be put on it perhaps 20 times, before one is satisfied. Practice and experience are the best guides here. The model itself will be naked in the first place, and for good results there should be a living model to work from. . . . In Rome there are girls who earn their living by posing for artists; others, whether from bashfulness or because they are women, will offer only their head, throat, nape of the neck, arms and hands as models for studies. The German customs, climate and code of propriety combine to prevent this, and to open so many locks it is often necessary to resort to Jupiter's strategem with Danae. . . .

The working of marble needs many years' practice, and if a statue were to be made by only one worker it would exhaust anyone's patience; so the task is divided between three men, each with his own speciality. The first is the one already mentioned, who 'points' the work with the help of plumb-lines; this gives a rough-hewn shape, like a snowman. The second, a real artist, strips off the bark, as it were; the limbs of the figure are cut out and separated by him; he uses various types of drill for this purpose and for scooping out the deep folds in the clothing. The third, and most venturesome, is responsible for smoothing the skin, putting the last touches to the hair, giving final shape to the features – shaping the eyelids with the chisel is the most difficult operation here – finishing the hands and feet, and putting the final bloom on the whole work, which requires a sensitive touch even in polishing.

Hosmer writes her thanks

Harriet Hosmer arrived in Rome from Ohio in the United States of America to study with the English neo-classical sculptor John Gibson. At first her father paid for her studies, but he suffered a financial reverse and in 1854 could no longer afford to support her. Wayman Crow, a friend of the family stepped in.

This is Harriet Hosmer's thank you letter. It has the special interest of describing how a sculptor managed the various material problems which formed part of the profession, complementing Schadow's letter written fifty years before.

(to Wayman Crow)[13] Rome, Oct. 12, 1854

Dear Mr Crow:
On returning last night I found your letter waiting for me. Indeed, I frankly confess that I don't know what to say, except that it seems a God's providence and that it has relieved my mind of a burden. The fact is that at the time of my 'bankruptcy' I was in debt. I had two or three bills coming due for marble, and at the same time had to apply for work already going on. It is very true that when one has a name, sculpture is a mine of wealth, but it is equally true that, name or no name, one must spend a good deal of money before one can hope to make one. Now, as I said in my last letter, I have spent money with too little thought, but no one has an idea of how expensive an affair it is, at first. You, dear Mr Crow, know that one must have a good capital to begin business at all, much more to begin with advantage. It is exactly the same thing in sculpture. A painter has no expense of the kind; he buys his canvas and his paints, which cost little and he is made; but from the time a sculptor begins, he finds that without funds he is at a standstill. Some seem to think that statues can be made like rail-fences. I do not agree with them. It is work, work, work, and if they would try their hands at it, they would become aware of the length of time one must study, before one can hope to do anything. Sometimes I cannot help thinking that too much is expected of me in so short a time as I have been here. Why, it is not three years yet, and what is that for learning so difficult an art in, an art which requires years and years to master? And when we consider that the first year I was kept copying the antique, it leaves rather a short time for me to have made my fortune in, as I am afraid I was expected to do. My master is the one to know if I have made progress, and he is satisfied with me, and is not easily satisfied either.

Now, dear mr Crow, I dare say you will say, 'What is the girl driving at?' Why, simply this, that you have understood my case well enough to lay me under an obligation, so great that if I were to realize your fondest hopes of me, I could never repay you. One thing is past denial, that however successful I may become in my profession, it is to you I owe all. The great thing in every profession, and most certainly so in art, is to get a good 'start', as we yankees say, and then all is right. But without this good start, I want to know what a young artist is to do? One may model till one is blind, and if one gets no commission for one's works, what is the use of it, for a work can never be really finished till it is in marble. I need not complain. When I look around and see other artists who have been here for years and are still waiting for a 'start' and then think what a friend I have in you, *sensa complimenti*, I wonder why I have been more blessed than my neighbours. Every successful artist in Rome, who is living, or who has ever lived, owes his success to *his* Mr Crow. The Duke of Devonshire was Mr. Gibson's, Mr. Hope was Thorwaldsen's. And I never read the life of any artist who did not date the rising of his lucky star from the hand of some beneficent friend or patron. You know the world pretty well, and therefore know that people in general wait for someone to lead the way, and then they are ready to follow, but the one to lead the way is not sent to every poor soul who wants it. It is very inspiring, too, to know that there is somebody who has great faith in you. You seem to work up to that faith and you do the very best you can, not to disappoint the one who hopes so much from you. I don't want to be 'puffed up with my own conceit', as the Bible has it, but at the same time I am determined that you shall not be wholly disappointed in me. I don't mean that you shall say, five or ten years hence, 'Well, I expected that girl would do something, but she never has.' If I have the use of my legs and arms, I will show you I haven't arms in vain. I am not very easily cast down, but have great faith, too, as well as yourself, and I have received a lesson, which I shall not forget, and which will do me a vast deal of good. . . .

Watts and his colourman

Science developed new colours for artists through the nineteenth century. A leading English businessman with a thorough knowledge of chemistry was Henry Newton, who took care and a personal interest in advising artists about materials and technique. Winsor and Newton, the firm he founded, is happily still going strong.

Newton had an extensive correspondence with George Frederick Watts; the artist's large allegorical pictures are at present less admired than his portraits. Watts was keenly interested in technical questions, and some hundreds of letters were exchanged between the two men.

(from H C Newton to G F Watts)[14] Crouch Oak, Addlestone
Surrey, July 28th, 1878

Dear Sir,

In reply to your favour of the 26th just to hand, on the subject of your rubbing your pictures over with the juice of potatoes or of onions, I do not think it likely that any oil-colour, however delicate, could be damaged by so doing. But I think it just possible that the farina left on the surface of a picture might affect the gloss of the varnish that might be applied after the picture is finished, unless the superfluous fecula were washed off. . . .

Watts replied as follows.

Dear Sir,

I must apologise for delaying so long to answer your interesting and instructive letter and thank you for so promptly sending me the information I asked for. I have been out of town, which must be my excuse. I think from what you say that the potato may be safely used. I like the dullness produced by its application, which, I suppose, would be completely got rid of by repeatedly oiling or varnishing. I have but lately come to the same conclusion you appear to have arrived at respecting the laying on of the colours. I am certain they should be applied as frankly as possible; what will not do should be removed, and replaced by fresh colour at the time, or allowed to dry thoroughly and be frankly repainted. No tormenting of the colour can result in good effects. I think, too, the colour should be used as dry as may be convenient, which will enable one to put it on crisply, the last painting being applied with plenty of oil (poppy I think the best) or the whole picture well soaked with oil when finished to prevent it from perishing. I wish you would kindly give me your opinion on this mode of work. Of course, I mean with reference to the safety. – Yours very truly and obliged, G. F. Watts.

Gauguin pleads poverty

Whether to paint thick or thin in oil paint was not altogether a question of preference. In the following extract Paul Gauguin replies to a suggestion that he should use more paint to create opulent effects in his Tahitian scenes. This comes from a letter addressed to his loyal Parisian friend Daniel de Monfried.

(to Daniel de Monfried)[15]

Plenty of colour, you say . . . but with what money could I afford it, if I was prodigal with colours? You can see that there are metres of canvas to cover. Besides, working in impasto is very dangerous if you go quickly; in a hot country especially one has to apply colour carefully and often, as it dries, otherwise you get mud. And then, I would paint a third of the number of pictures; at the price that paintings sell . . . I think on the whole that time, and varnish, will greatly improve my pictures. Moreover on my first trip my canvases were much less rich in paint and I do not think they are the worse for that.

Costa advises a novice

Giovanni Costa was fortunate in finding friends and a market for his painting in England, since his involvement in the liberation of Italy made him an exile from Rome. He served on Garibaldi's staff, and fought at Mentana in the insurrection of 1867. It was in 1886 that he and some Italian colleagues founded an exhibiting society whose name incorporated Costa's ruling passions, *In Arte Libertas*.

This letter to a beginner explains his own practice, in particular how he arrived at tonal compositions.

(to an unknown correspondent)

You will take, dear colleague, a white canvas, or non-absorbent panel spotless as your soul, and you will rub the surface over with nimium, taking care that it can be even all over. On this surface you will very carefully draw your design with a pen, or steel point, taking care that no great alterations be necessary later on. Then divide the strip values of your composition, starting from the background with simple and opaque colours, and working forward with others gradually more transparent, till you reach the actual foreground, for which you use the surface of nimium lade on white. After this, you will work at the modelling and chiaroscuro in a monotone colour of your choice. I have always made use of burnt umber, red, cobalt, and white lead. The modelling must be well felt and strong, so as to be able to stand the layer of local colour. As you see, you will now have the design, the chiaroscuro, the modelling, the colour. What is lacking? Light. Before putting it in, you will work with gray for the values, mindful that this, when dry, will have to be sure as basis for all the half-tints. And now you will put in the light, for which you will avoid yellow, but make use of white, black and red: and by working over this by stabbing you will make the half-tints of the ground tell out; and finally when all is dry, you will give yourself up to the pleasure of finishing the picture with scumbles, adding yellow to complete the colour – worshipping God, *Maxima cum laetitia in coro et organo in cimbalis bene somantibus.*

Do not let all this make you forget that it is sentiment which must come before everything, in the midst of everything, after everything. In the first place the study, the offspring of sentiment and love, must give birth to the work of art; afterwards, we shall have to think of the babe, and the education of the child.

Certainly, sentiment united to technical knowledge will be more powerful than without it, just as a hand well armed is more powerful than that of a savage with his nails for sole defence.

3

Personal Lives

A monograph on an artist usually has little space for personal detail, which is understandably crowded out by facts about art and its interpretations. Even biographies often do not print the full text of letters, only using such quotations as fit the author's narrative. Many readers look to fiction to supply the missing story, or even to films; but everyone knows that such sources tend to be long on emotion but short on accuracy. First-hand evidence about artists' lives and their circumstances can, however, be found in letters, which can thus be useful correctives to myths.

Sometimes an artist may seem almost within reach. It is easy to sympathise with the alarm of a young artist newly married in the artists' colony at Grez-sur-Loing when faced with the arrival of August Strindberg, who had published his novel *The Red Room* about the Stockholm art world four years before. Here is part of a letter that Karin Larsson wrote to her mother in 1883.

> Oh, mother mine, pray for me!
>
> Strindberg is coming!
>
> Eva Bonnier and her sister are coming here any day now! A couple of days ago we had Mr and Mrs Skredsvig, a sweet woman, intelligent and gifted. How do you think I can make out with such company?
>
> Do you think Carl might disapprove of me?
>
> You write that I should be natural and at ease. But there is an art in that, when one becomes so embarrassed as to

> get stiff and scared. You drop everything, bump into the corners of things, and step on people's toes. My heart is in my mouth when I think about it.[1]

The Larssons were living and working abroad; but soon afterwards they returned to Sweden to live in Dalarna, where their house became famous through Carl Larsson's drawings of their delightful home and family life. This chapter looking at artists' personal lives starts with the household of a French animal painter.

Households

Bonheur's birds and animals

Rosa Bonheur made her reputation as a painter of animal subjects in the 1850s. An early success in Paris was a painting called 'A Horse Fair', shown at the Salon, which sold well as an engraving, and of which the artist did two replicas. Her fame was ensured by the astute management of her career by Ernest Gambart, her dealer and friend.

The artist's love of birds and animals was unusually comprehensive. Two letters provide evidence of her arrangements and her affections.

(to Auguste Cain)[2] 1885

I wanted to write to you sooner that the villainous little parrots, which you have been kind enough to give me, have arrived in perfect health. The sight of the verdure has given them matrimonial ideas and I write to ask you to have me made a small nest, as soon as possible. I have a big cage that I have put them in temporarily. By the way, if I remember rightly, your cage is a brass one. If you haven't ordered mine, I should prefer an iron one, but of the same shape and size as yours. The plumage of my pretty little creatures has become most beautiful under the influence of the air, no doubt. They may fly about as they please. When you come, you will see what good care I take of them.

You know that the soup of friendship and the rabbit of fraternity are always awaiting you. So come without ceremony, whenever you feel inclined.

You ask the price of my drawing. It is 2,000 francs. It is now at the picture framer's.

(to Auguste Cain) April 27, 1881

I have just heard from M. Manger, who announces the arrival of the male chamois he had promised, to replace the other one he sent and which reached me, half dead. I think he is an honest man, who himself was taken in. As you kindly promised to examine this one, I let you know at once of its arrival. I enclose the letter, stating the price – 416 francs. The other cost me 500 francs, which of course I have lost. Now, the essential thing is that the animal should be in good condition and not too wild. Please keep this letter, for I shan't pay, this time, until the chamois is definitely installed, safe and sound, in my park.

The following passage supplements these letters, though its provenance is not clear.

. . . 'My poor lioness can't move; she is going to die.' A few minutes later, I heard a velvet-soft step down in the hall. I went to see what it was, and found that it was my lioness, who, though dying, had made an effort to see me again for the last time. She knew I had gone upstairs. She heard my voice and had crawled on to the stairs in order to reach me. I went down a little way and she stopped. When I came to her, I took her into my arms and stroked her. She lay back and looked at me like a person who thinks, and died thus gazing at me. I believe in the good God and in his Paradise for the just, but I do not approve of everything in religion. For instance, I find it monstrous that animals should be said to have no soul. My lioness loved. She, therefore, had more soul than certain people who do not love.

From an artistic colony

One domestic solution to an artist's need for breaking with a conventional mode of living was to join an artists' colony. Two examples are the group at Pont Aven where Gauguin and his friends worked, or the international community at Grez where the Larssons were in the 1880s. Worpswede was the community which Paula Becker chose, the beauty of the place especially appealing to her. In her diary in 1897 she wrote:

> Birches, birches, pines and old willows. Beautiful brown moors, exquisite brown! Canals with black reflections, asphalt black. The Hamme with its dark sails. It's a wonderland, a land of the gods. I take pity on this beautiful piece of earth whose inhabitants don't know how beautiful it is. You tell them but they do not understand.[3]

(to her family)[3] Worspwede, 25 November 1898

Dearests,

. . . meanwhile I go on living and drawing, drawing, drawing. I long for the time when I am able to do what I'd like to do now. I really have a gigantic wildcat of a hangover from painting, the biggest of my life so far. Such creatures seem to thrive and grow strong in artistic climates. But the climate is considerate enough to permit other sensitive, special moods to enrich my life: a sunset with pealing bells; a visit to an old woman with one foot in the grave, whose thoughts flare brightly one last time before the great catastrophe. In the beautiful, powerful language of the people she spoke to me, in a breath half giving-out, of birth and marriage and death. Whenever these people have something to say you listen to them transfixed. But most of them speak only in platitudes, only empty words, in order to talk at all. It's terrible and makes them seem so ignorant.

Now is the season of the spinning room. The old women go from house to house with their spinning wheels. Then the men process the wool into stockings. Even my Garwes knits in his spare time.

I love most going to old Renkin ''hind the firs' (they're pines). He makes brooms, gossips amusingly, and rocks his grandchild on his lap, tirelessly singing 'Ooaa, ooaa' to her on two notes. When her young mother said with a mischievous look, 'She knows that song by now', he immediately made up something new, 'Aaoo, aaoo.' These people have such heartfelt affection for each other, a rarity here, and they let the larger world be – which for them is simply Worpswede, Worpswede.

My evening nude makes me very happy. Even though the little girl is knock-kneed, she moved with such naive grace. Mackensen had her take about twenty different poses today. I would have liked to have held on to every single one of them.

I'm reading Bismarck's letters. The great man becomes very human.

When he speaks about huntsmanship, women and his impressions of nature he shades into Uncle Wulf for me. Bismarck, *Werther*, Marie Bashkirtseff, Worpswede, all in one little head. I seem strange to myself here. I look at the bustle of life as if from the dress-circle, and, given where I am sitting, I don't think much about how it affects me. Till now one played a pretty big role on one's little stage. Now the play is over. One simply is. One advances and draws back without being bothered by an audience. Occasionally one's vanity longs for a little boost, a boost that only the world can give. Even if it's just a kick, at least one feels important enough to be kicked. It's seldom and not in the best moments one longs for nothing at all.

Family and friends

A quiet solitude

The romantic and poetic landscapes of Caspar David Friedrich were securely grounded in his religious faith, of which there is a hint in the following letter. Meanwhile he gives some pleasant vignettes of his solitary and meditative life.

(to his wife Karoline)[4] Dresden, the 10th July, 1822

Dear Liene,

If I were to describe to you in every detail all the things I have said and done the whole day long you would receive as my letter a huge sheet of blank paper. Everything is quiet, quiet, quietness all around me; this quietness is doing me good, but I would not like to have it round me to such a high degree all the time. I eat my breakfast alone (for some days Wilhelm has been drinking tea at home). I have lunch and supper alone, and always alone; it does me good but I would not wish to have it this way all the time. In the evenings I go out into the fields and furrows with the blue sky above and the green shoots and trees beside me, and then I am not alone; for He who created heaven and earth surrounds me and His love supports me, as it supports you and indeed all of you in the little village.

When the weather became stormy on Saturday I was quite concerned about you, but I was glad that you all survived on board ship and without undue anxiety.

In the large garden there is quite a sizable patch of grass burnt away, not from the sun but as a result of a fire. Fire engines came from Strahlen to put it out.

I am in good health and spirits, as I trust you are. I hope you and Emma are bathing a lot. Write often and soon.

Our doves are busy sitting on their eggs, the males more than the females.

I nearly forgot the most important thing: I shan't be in Meissen for your birthday, so it would be better to postpone the little sponge-cakes to another time. Nature offers so many delicious foods at the moment that I believe one can quite easily do without artificial foods, which, besides, only harm the stomach . . .

Fuseli begs a friend to stay

Some artists wrote lively letters to their friends, remembering the past or hoping to meet. Here is a letter of persuasion to stay at Somerset House, then the home of the Royal Academy. The writer is the painter Henry Fuseli, who held office as the Academy's Keeper and had accommodation there. Fuseli was Swiss by birth, a good classicist and linguist, and much respected by his colleagues and students. He often had a *bon mot*, calling for an umbrella in front of one of Constable's pictures of a shower of rain, and admitting that Blake was 'damned good to steal from' for visionary themes, the subjects of many of his own pictures. He is writing to the friend who became his biographer.

(to John Knowles)[5] Somerset House, September 12, 1817

To any other person an apology might be necessary; to you, whose friendship can neither be heated or cooled by correspondence or silence, I despise offering any: if by remaining mute, I have deprived myself of one sense of pleasure, it has reserved to me another, when we meet: your letter made *me* happy, because you could not have written it, had you not been so *yourself*.

Hammond has perhaps told you that I went to Luton with him and Roscoe: I spent some happy hours there; and, of course, but few. Since my return, I have been riding or crawling in a kind of daylight-somnambulism between this place, Brompton and Putney-hill. Whether I shall continue to do so the remainder of the month, or go to snuff in some sea air, will depend on my wife's success or disappointment at Cheltenham.

The chief reason why I send you this scrawl, is to offer you a bed here on your return, on the same floor with myself, and a chamber as pleasant and well furnished as my own, viz. with demigods and beauties. I earnestly request you to accept of it, and not persist in the foolhardy resolution of sleeping in a newly painted room. If Hammond is obliged to have his house painted, pray oblige me with your compliance, and, in giving me the preference, you will be at home, and your brother can surely not except against it, considering the distance at which he lives. I will not take a refusal.

I feel my head so stupid, my hand so disobedient, my pen so execrable, my ink such a mudpond, that I ought to save you the trouble of deciphering more. Adieu, love me as I do you, neither more nor less, and hasten your return. Ever, Henry Fuseli.

Bewick makes amends

Thomas Bewick carried out his work as a wood engraver at Cherryburn, now a museum in his honour, just north of Newcastle-upon-Tyne; but in his youth he had been apprenticed to Isaac Taylor in London.

Towards the end of his life, Taylor visited Newcastle, but without seeing his former pupil. Bewick decided to send him a copy of his famous publication, *British Birds*, which he accompanied with this respectful letter.

(to Isaac Taylor)[6] Newcastle 18th April, 1806

Dear Sir

After the slipping away of nearly twenty-nine years, in the whole time never having seen or heard of you, it may be supposed that I have forgotten you, and no doubt you have had but little occasion to remember me, except it be to think upon the great pains you took to serve me while I remained in London, and that I have never acknowledged the sense I entertain of the obligation – but long as is the period since I had my last interview with you, I have never in all that time thought about London without turning over your name in my mind and coupling it with the plans you then laid for my advancement. But those plans were not to take place and those times have passed away.

I was then in the heyday of youth, completely like a wild colt, and from the temperate, or rather from the poor, manner in which I had too long habituated myself to live, I became too independent – regardless of money-making and fearless as to the future, and as I did not like London, viewing it perhaps too much on the gloomy side of the picture, no considerations of what it might have done for me could tempt me to remain in it.

I now, as a token of respect and gratitude, beg your acceptance of these two volumes of *British Birds* – these books may be of little value to you, but I know not what I can do more. If they can in any degree serve to put you in mind of your own great goodness of heart, that consideration will always be gratifying to me.

These publications were brought forth after many a long night's labour, for the greater part of the cuts was done by candlelight, when left in my workshop alone, and chiefly on account of my being uninterrupted at that time. I hope the reward of a small independence will at last come, and if it does it will come opportunely, for I have abused my sight so much that I cannot now continue long at engraving. In other respects I am strong, hearty and well. I hope this will find you in health and spirits.

I am, my dear Sir, with the greatest respect, your grateful and obedient servant, Thomas Bewick.

Constable well-employed in town

John Constable's easy style in personal letters is at its best when writing to intimates. In 1822 his wife was in Brighton for her health, but Constable stayed in London, where he wrote a letter in diary form to her. The following are extracts.[7]

Tuesday 15 June: . . . On getting to work, Fisher called and we met as usual delighted with each other. We chatted a great deal, and then went down to the Exhibition. Returned to dinner, boiled mutton and some nice sherry . . . Fisher's sisters are returned from Paris quite pleased.

Wednesday, 16 June: After dinner a French gentleman and lady called, Monsieur le Vicomte de Thulusson, to beg permission to see '*de* Gallery of Mr Constable'. They were in a nice English coach. He was much pleased. Could talk a little English and we got on very well – a genteel young man, and the lady was very pretty and genteel – they seemed a most amiable and elegant pair – so quietly and truly the gentlefolks. He ordered a little picture and wish to know if I would accept any commission from Paris – I said, certainly.

He said I was much known and esteemed at Paris, & if I would come I should be made much of – & he hoped I should call on him. The artists would receive me 'with great éclat'. He was wholly struck with the picture of Tinney's – which now looks so very beautiful on the easel. It is of service to me to have so good a work to show.

Thursday, 17 June: Came home and set to work on Fisher's picture – which I did very well . . . About half past one Fisher called. We had a nice leg of mutton ready at two, and after dinner and a glass or two of sherry we set off for Pall Mall, to the Gallery, & looked in at Christies. We saw there all Reinagle's collection of pictures and some copies by his son. We then went to the New gallery – beautiful rooms but the most wretched display of pictures that it is possible to conceive – nothing in the world can be worse.

Constable's wife enjoyed his account, and replied.

Saturday 19 June: I have no treat like your journal and letters . . . I hardly allow myself to wish for you, knowing how well and profitably you are employed, but I endeavour to make myself happy, as the separation is for our mutual good, but when you do come, I trust we shall enjoy our rides and walks. I think there is nothing more interesting than the flying shadows on the downs . . .

An entry about the success of Constable's paintings shown in Paris is dated 22 June:

Had a letter from Paris. Mr Arrowsmith informed me of the safe arrival of the pictures and how much they were admired. The letter shall be sent to you – he talks of coming again in the end of this month. I shall be ready for him. His letter is quite flattering, but I hope not to go to Paris as long as I live. I do not see any way it is going to answer.

Turner retails the Roman gossip

J. M. W. Turner was not a loquacious letter-writer, but his comments could be sharply to the point. He enjoyed turning a phrase or two; his reply to one invitation was: 'sorry to say I am engaged out of town today so I must be put down on the Black list, instead of the Brown Sherry'.

Turner's exceptionally early election as an Academician at the age of twenty-seven meant that he was informed about art politics almost all his life. In the following letter he gives a commentary about life in Rome, and the sculpture in progress for the forthcoming Royal Academy. His correspondent, being a sculptor, probably enjoyed Turner's wit at John Gibson's expense.

(to Francis Chantrey)[8] No 12 Piazza Mignanelli Rome
Nov. 6. 1828

My dear Chantrey

I intended long before this (but you will say Fudge) to have written; but even now very little information have I to give you in matters of Art, for I have confined myself to the painting department at Corso; and having finished *one*, am about the second, and getting on with Lord E's, which I began the very first touch at Rome; but as folk here talked that I would show them *not*, I finished a small three feet four to stop their gabbing: so now to business.

Sculpture, of course, first, for it carries away all the patronage, so it is said, in Rome; but all seem to share in the goodwill of the patrons of the day. Gott's studio is full. Wyatt and Rennie, Ewing, Buxton, all employed. Gibson has two groups in hand, 'Venus and Cupid', and 'The Rape of Hylas', three figures very forward, though I doubt much if it will be in time (taking the long voyage into the scale) for the Exhibition, though it is for England. Its style is something like 'The Psyche', being two standing figures of nymphs leaning, enamoured, over the young Hylas, with his pitcher. The Venus is a sitting figure, with the Cupid in attendance; if it had wings like a dove, to flee away and be at rest, the rest would not be worse for the change. Thorwaldsen is closely engaged on the late Pope's monument. Portraits of the superior animal, man, is to be found in all. In some the inferior – viz. greyhounds and poodles, cats and monkeys, &c. & . . .

Pray give my remembrances to Jones and Stokes, and tell *him* I have not seen a bit of coal stratum for months. My love to Mrs Chantrey, and take the same and good wishes of

Yours most truly
J. M. W. Turner

A dark and blighting cloud

A tragic story is told in a sad letter from Ellen Sharples about the death of her daughter from cancer, and the subsequent death of her son. Her correspondent was Harriet Pigott, author of *Records of Real Life in the Palace and the Cottage.*

Ellen Sharples' own career had a long span in two continents from the 1790s in America when, as we shall see, she had begun copying her husband's portrait drawings; she died in England at Clifton, Bristol, a generous benefactor to the West of England Academy, in March 1849.

(to Miss Pigott)[9]

My dear Rolinda just as she was attaining perfection in her favorite art, a dark and blighting cloud suddenly threw its sombre shadow over all. A considerable induration in the right breast was perceived, the first manifestation of that most dreadful of all diseases, a cancer. The skill and attention of surgeons to arrest its progress were unavailing; after various experiments, operation was finally advised, but opposed by Sir Astley Cooper. In a few months commenced a long and painful illness, born with a heroism beyond human nature . . . On the night of Feb.10 1838 to our inexpressible anguish she departed as if falling into a gentle and peaceful sleep . . . The loss of a beloved sister was as great a trial to my dear son as the loss of a beloved daughter to his mother . . . He executed a variety of beautiful drawings for me to present to Rolinda's many friends as slight tokens of acknowledgement for their great kindnesses . . . For many years his health had been delicate and in Lower Harley Place he had an alarming cough. The removal to St. Vincent's Parade proved beneficial . . . his general health had improved and there was every reason to hope that all danger was past. This hope proved fallacious as other hopes had done before. Late in the autumn of 1838 the cough returned and continued . . . weakness and emaciation became more and more perceptible . . . and on the tenth of August when he departed a year and a half after his sister, the dreadful blow was almost too much for me to sustain.

Keene gains an understanding

Life as an illustrator was unpredictable, and so were the rewards. Charles Keene, black and white illustrator well known for his *Punch* drawings, was able to achieve fame and wealth. He also was accorded the respect of artists both in Britain and France, Delacroix and Whistler being among his admirers. His success may be contrasted with the unlucky circumstances of some of his French contemporaries such as Joseph Travies who died in poverty, or Grandville who wrote his own sad epitaph; 'Here lies Grandville; he gave life to everything and made everything move and speak. The one thing is, he didn't know how to make his own way.'

By 1884, Keene had realised he ought to be more careful about disposing of his drawings, as is demonstrated by the following exchange of letters. His friend had supplied an idea for a drawing and asked Keene to give it to him.

(to A. W. Tuer)[10] February 14, 1884

Dear Tuer,

Let us have an understanding. These original drawings are my poor 'stock-in-trade' – my capital – my copyrights, etc. Do you wish to purchase this sketch as a matter of business? If you want a replica of this in particular I'll make one and give it you with pleasure in this case, but I can't undertake to do it always. I bought a relic of old Bewick at the sale – John's walking-stick that T.B. always used after his brother's death. The books went at an inordinate price.

Yours, Charles S. Keene

(to Charles Keene) February 15, 1884

Your letter was a shock indeed, my dear Keene, but I am glad it was written. Your good opinion is worth more to me than all the drawings you ever did put together, and it's a sad thing that this miserable misunderstanding should have been going on for years. I always understood – how I got it into my stupid old head I do not know – that you considered an original contribution that you could accept for 'Punch' as a *quid pro quo* for your original sketch. I don't think that I was even aware at first that you ever disposed of your drawings. I simply felt proud to possess *your* drawings of *my* little jokes. On looking over the sketches that I have, I find that I supplied matter for all except three – one you gave me, one you gave my wife, and the other I took as a matter of business. 'Let us have an understanding,' you say, and I earnestly say AMEN to that; so do please put me right, for I am all at sea and dispirited. I am not dispirited about getting no more sketches. I would return what I have, but I know you would bundle them back by the next post.

Very faithfully yours, And. W. Tuer.

(to A. W. Tuer) Febuary 16, 1884

Dear Tuer,
I was sure I had only to tell you of this present little embarrassment (there has been none between us hitherto, believe me) to make it clear to you. I have given away no end of these drawings, and shall do, I daresay, and would like to give them all, but, in fact, I have sold a great many to friends, and this is the most imperative reason for my looking at them as of any value; besides, I have never insured my life, as I ought to have done, and have been brought to take heed of them on this account; so I hope you won't think me greedy or selfish on speaking out to you on the matter openly. I have not got back the drawing of the Groom and the Doctor yet. You ought to see them before you take them, and I'll forward them to you if you like, and I ask five guineas each if you take them, and am,
Yours ever, Charles S. Keene.

Du Maurier recalls old times

A letter aiming at a reconciliation is from George Du Maurier to Edward Burne-Jones, whose retrospective exhibition was held at the New Gallery in 1893. Burne-Jones had disapproved of some of Du Maurier's *Punch* cartoons which he had felt were slighting to Rossetti. There had been some coldness between the two friends, but they made up their differences.

(to Burne-Jones)[11] February 1893

My dear Burne-Jones, I went yesterday to the New Gallery. It was a peculiar sensation of pleasure – *très doux et un peu triste* – like opening an old diary. I knew all or very nearly all the pictures there, remembering well where and when I had seen them, and with what impressions. It reminded me of Millais' show at the Grosvenor Gallery, where you were so enthusiastic – do you recollect? We went down Bond Street afterwards in a four-wheeler together and you nearly stamped through the floor! Millais' Autumn Leaves, the Vale of Rest, – at Christie's – what a pleasure it was to see them again after so many years! And in just the same way I can't tell you with what pleasure I saw Merlin and Nimue, the Merciful Knight, Circe and her black panther, and others I had so loved in the happy days of youth: and found that absence had only made the heart grow fonder!

The original Tess of the d'Urbervilles

Hamo Thornycroft, the son of two sculptor parents, was himself responsible for many public monuments. One of his close friends was Sir Edmund Gosse, the literary critic, who features in the following letter.

(to his wife)[12] May 8th, 1894

Dearest one,

My happiest hours are always in some way related to you and for this reason I now at this late hour am drawn to my writing desk to give you an anecdote which I heard from Gosse an hour ago and which has given me a sort of elation at a time when dull sleep would, if I were alone, have overtaken me . . .

He said on Friday last at the private view of the Academy he met

a distinguished novelist wandering solitary through the galleries looking somewhat tired and ill. In reply to Gosse's remarks thereon the novelist said: 'No, I am not so tired now, I am better than I was earlier in the day for I have been cheered up by seeing the most beautiful woman in England, or rather her whom I think the most beautiful woman in England, her on whom I thought when I wrote Tess of the d'Urbervilles.' 'And who was that?' said Gosse. 'Why, it was Mrs. Hamo Thornycroft' said Thomas Hardy.
Now, is not that a nice little story and true?
Your ever loving Hamo T.

Children

Menzel gives a reprimand
The fame of Adolf Menzel as a painter and illustrator of the history of Prussia centres on his depiction of the life of Frederick the Great; in the twentieth century he has been perhaps as much admired for his interiors and pictures of street life, whose originality of treatment is seen as foreshadowing Impressionism.

When he was enlisted to advise the son of a friend on his progress in art, Menzel was frank.

(to Carl Arnold, the son of Menzel's friend, C H Arnold)[13]

Berlin, June 4th, '52

My dear Carlchen,
So that you will not be 'mad as hell' at me again, I will, as you will shortly see, treat the subject of yourself on paper. From your personal description recently sent to me, I see with satisfaction that you certainly go around every day as a well-combed, washed and tidy young person. One may likewise assume that your previously dubious brown attire has changed colour to that definitely gaudy hue which in olden times was known as caca du Dauphin. To say nothing of the regulation teatime peasant-style cravat.

Tell me, how could you not see for yourself that this failure of a piece was the least suitable work for me to be able to judge your progress in the last six months? In the interests of your own honour I believe you have produced better work during this time, so why did you not send me some of it? Instead you send such a thing where it is obvious that you did not bother to correct the basic mistakes which crept in at the beginning. You have tried to put them right later and have laboured till you were quite feeble and crippled. If, as I describe, this is not the way things happened, then it is even more unpardonable. Just look at the position of the eyes, the mouth, the whole head indeed! The nose is the only tolerable feature. The lack of likeness and the stiff posture I do not condemn – with reflected images there are very difficult precipices to negotiate, particularly for one of your tender years.

But a reprimand is deserved for the utterly tasteless hair, dull and devoid of ornament. How could you not feel revulsion when you stood back and looked at the painting? On the top of that it is not true to life; your hair has quite different accents. The same is true of the skin, pinkish and green. In brief take note of this: if the organic composition is defective then over-attention to detail results in a mess of brushstrokes, and that is the hallmark of a dilettante.

You must set about the next picture quite differently. May God help you!

Haydon and the deaf girl

Artists were frequently asked to help in instructing young people, sometimes members of the family or family friends. The charming letter that follows is one of many pieces of evidence that could be given of the generosity of artists.

(to Elizabeth)[14] 19th October, 1841

My dearest Elizabeth,

I am very happy to hear from you; and if you will send up your drawings to me, I will always correct them and send them back. You shall have your drawing book in a few days, as soon as I have time to get it. Make yourself, my dear Elizabeth, mistress of drawing, because, though God has deprived you of hearing, He has blessed you with sight, the greatest blessing of all the senses; and if you will cultivate drawing, you will never have an irksome moment, and you will never care about hearing. I assure you many people would be glad to be deaf sometimes, they hear such disagreeable things. You cannot put your hands to your ears, for that would be rude, but you can shut your eyes in a moment if you do not like to see anything offensive.

I know a good man whom God has deprived of hearing; but he had good eyes, and he studied drawing, and drew beautifully, and he was the happiest man in the world, as you will be the happiest woman, if you learn to draw. Don't draw nonsense; but draw the human head, and face, and eyes, and then you will be able to draw your good papa and mama, and sister and brother, and that will make you and them very happy.

Trust in God, my dear little friend, and pray to Him every night and every morning, and feel grateful for the many blessings you enjoy in spite of the one affliction He has been pleased to give you. You will find, after all, that you will remember Him more, and pray to Him oftener, and be more blessed than other people who are able to hear everything – and yet forget Him all their lives.

Kind regards to papa and mama.

Your affectionate friend, B. R. Haydon.

Toulouse-Lautrec writes to his grandmother

Henri de Toulouse-Lautrec in the following letter is writing dutifully as a twelve-year-old to his paternal grandmother. He mentions the artist Princeteau, under whom he first studied, and signs himself with the chic English spelling of his Christian name.

(to Mme R. C. de Toulouse-Lautrec)[15] Paris January 1876

My dear Grandma,

I regret very much not being able to wish you a Happy New Year in person. I haven't been as lucky as my cousins in spending vacations at Bosc. I haven't any idea when I shall be able to see you again; I hope it will be as soon as possible. I have been having a good time during the Christmas holiday and hope the same for the New Year's. I have been with Mama to see M. Princeteau's big picture showing Washington on horseback. He is going to send it to the big exhibition in America. For Christmas I have bought a beautiful book, drawn by *Crafty*, on the Zoological Gardens. The falconer Papa admires so much is in Ireland just now and I am consoling myself with my friend Toby.

Goodby, my dear Grandma. I'm not very good at letter-writing, but I love you very much and kiss you with all my heart, wishing you a happy and prosperous New Year.
Your respectful grandson Henry de T-Lautrec

4

ART AND EXHIBITIONS

One of the functions of the Academies, as we have seen, was to act as teaching institutions. They were also responsible for staging exhibitions. As the century saw an immense increase in artistic activity, this was reflected in the large official shows organised by the Academies, and as the decades passed these were supplemented by other exhibitions organised by rival societies, by individual shows, and the activities of dealers.

Selecting work for exhibitions was notoriously difficult, and the choices made were often controversial. Zola gives a description of the process of selection for the Paris Salon in his realistic novel *L'Oeuvre*, which can set the scene for us.

> This committee work was a really hard task, and even Bongrand's strong legs grew tired. The work was cut out every day by the assistants, an endless row of large pictures resting on the ground, leaning against the hand-rails, and stretching away through the galleries of the first floor, right round the Palace; and every afternoon, at one o'clock precisely, the forty committee-men, headed by their president, equipped with a bell, started off on the same promenade, until all the initial letters of the alphabet had been exhausted. They gave their decisions standing; the work was got through as fast as possible, the worst canvases being rejected without going to the vote; at times, however, discussions delayed the party, there was a ten-

minutes quarrel, and the picture which had caused the dispute was reserved for the evening revision, while two men, holding a cord ten metres long, stretched it tightly at a distance of four paces from the line of pictures, so as to keep back the flood of committee-men, who pushed each other in the heat of the dispute, and whose stomachs, despite everything, would bend the cord. Behind the committee-men marched the seventy museum-keepers in white blouses, executing their evolutions under the orders of a brigadier, and sorting the pictures at each decision communicated by the secretaries, the accepted paintings being separated from the rejected ones, which were carried off and laid aside like corpses after a battle. And the round lasted during two mortal hours, without respite, without there being a chair to sit down upon; the committee-men had to remain all the while upon their legs, in a tired tramp, amid icy draughts, which compelled even the least chilly among them to bury themselves in the depths of their fur-lined coats. Thus the three o'clock snack was very welcome: half-an-hour's rest at a buffet where claret, chocolate, and sandwiches could be obtained. It was there that the market of mutual concessions was held, the bartering of influence and votes carried on. So that no one might be forgotten amid the hailstorm of applications which fell upon the committee-men, most of them had little notebooks, which they consulted; and they promised to vote for the exhibitors that a colleague protected on condition that this colleague voted for the ones whom they were interested in. Others, however, taking no part in these intrigues, either from austerity or indifference, finished smoking a cigarette, gazing vacantly about them.

Then the work began again, but more agreeably, in a gallery where there were chairs, even tables with pens and paper and ink. All the pictures which did not reach a metre and a half in height were judged there – 'passed on the easel', as the expression goes – being ranged, ten or twelve together, along a kind of trestle covered with green baize. A good many committee-men grew beatifically absent-minded on their seats, several wrote their letters, and the president had to get angry to obtain presentable majorities. Sometimes a gust of passion swept by; they all jostled each other; the votes, usually given by raising the hand, took place amid such feverish excitement that hats and walking sticks were waved about the tumultuous surging of heads.[1]

Official exhibitions

Farington speaks from experience

Joseph Farington was a Royal Academician active in art politicking. We learn almost more than we want to know about him because he kept a detailed diary, which includes such minutiae as table placings at dinner parties. He was a friend of Lawrence who was President of the Royal Academy when this letter was written in 1820.

The good standing of the Royal Academy, both in its teaching and its exhibitions, was Farington's constant concern. Was such an Academy possible for Ireland? Farington has views, quotes his experience, and concludes by adding a note of dismay about the behaviour of George IV's estranged wife.

(to Thomas Lawrence)[2] Woodvale, Oct 12th, 1820

. . . I have considered the proposal to establish a Royal Academy of Arts in Ireland and approve it. I regret that I am not in London at this time so far as this matter is an Object, as I have the means of giving you most particular information. I came to the Metropolis in 1763, and the Incorporated Society of Artists was instituted in 1765. I was afterwards a member, and know the whole history of it and also what relates to the foundation of the Royal Academy. Experience has proved that there is only one safe and lasting mode of forming such a Society. The great points are these. First the number of members shall consist of not more than 40 first-rate members, consisting of Painters, Sculptors, and Architects. This number to be filled up gradually according to rising merit. The Incorporated Society was soon a scene of contest and confusion, the consequence of admitting Engravers . . . and inferior artists, to an unlimited number, who by their quantity were enabled to outvote the really respectable members. This caused the most distinguished artists to withdraw their names and to apply to his majesty to patronise a new and select formation, which, wisely planned, has made the Royal Academy an object of high consideration throughout the Empire . . .

At the time the Incorporated Society was formed there existed an Old *established Academy* for drawing from *the Life* only, in Peter's Court, St Martin's Lane . . .

I thank you for your information respecting the Queen's business. My sentiments are hitherto unaltered. While abroad, she was a roving, careless, and I believe sensual wanderer and I am confirmed in this opinion by her conduct since she returned to England. Here she has been at least the mouth-piece of brutal railing and sedition, and has shown her mind to be devoid of principle and decorum. The evidence given for her for the most part does reflect little credit upon those who gave it. I think it often obviously false, and much of it shuffling . . .

Yrs most truly. Jos. Farington

Géricault scorns the critics

Theodore Géricault is here replying to a letter of congratulations about his picture, 'The Raft of the Medusa'. The subject was sensational because the shipwreck it depicts had been brought about by the incompetence of officers who should never have been appointed. Hence Géricault's comments about the Bourbon party, which the *Drapeau Blanc* supported.

(to M. Musigny)[3] 1819

I have received your kind letter, and can have nothing more urgent or better to do than answer it at once. Glory, seductive as you declare it to be and as I sometimes imagine it, does not yet entirely absorb me, and I devote much less care to it than that required by a true and amiable friendship. I am more flattered by your lines and your gratifying forecast of my success, than by all the articles in which insult and praise are dispensed with so much *sagacity.* Here the artist ranks with the comedian and must train himself to show complete indifference towards all that emanates from newspapers and their writers. The impassioned lover of true glory must look for it sincerely in what is beautiful and noble, and turn a deaf ear to the din raised by the pedlars of illusion.

This year our critics have reached the apex of absurdity. Every picture is judged first and foremost by the *spirit* in which it was composed. Thus, a liberal writer is to be heard praising a particular work for revealing a truly patriotic brush, a nationalist touch. The same work judged by an ultra becomes a mere revolutionary composition coloured throughout by sedition, the faces of all its figures bearing an expression of hatred for our fatherly government. A rag called the *Drapeau Blanc* even accused me of slandering the entire Admiralty by the expression of one of my faces. The poor creatures who write such imbecilities have no doubt never been through a two weeks' fast, for if they had they would know that neither poetry nor painting can convey the full horror of the situation into which the people on that raft were thrust.

There you have a sample of the glory that is to be heaped upon us here below, and of the guilty causes which may deprive us of it. Let us admit that it well deserves to be called the vanity of vanities. But I would not disdain that form of it which was dear to Pascal and which you also love.

Cordially yours, T. Géricault.

Constable fears he is misunderstood

Although Constable studied at the Royal Academy and exhibited there, he was disappointed at his late election to the rank of Royal Academician. There was considerable competition, and Constable was at a disadvantage since he was a landscape artist, not a history painter or a portraitist.

This letter to an Academician is in the artist's formal style, which reads very stiffly in comparison with his intimate letters. He mentions his wife's health for which he had serious reason to be anxious; she died later in the year. Constable's own election as a Royal Academician was in 1829; he said, 'It has been delayed until I am solitary and cannot impart it.'

(to Thomas Phillips, RA)[4] 6 Well Walk, Hampstead Feb. 2, 1828

My dear Sir
I cannot help writing to you to beg pardon in the first place for my (I fear) abrupt conversation with you yesterday, and to state other matters to you which relate to myself, and which I trust you will not take amiss.

It seemed to me that you had not formed wholly a right impression of myself. You thought I had been successful in public patronage, and besides, that I had not made those sacrifices to my art and to the Royal Academy that others of the Associates had done. May I be allowed under your candour to say a little about myself since I have been in the Academy? During that period I have painted about ten pictures (as considerable as my limited powers would go) all of which made their first appearance on its walls. One only of them (The Lock) found a purchaser among English collectors. It was sold to Mr Morrison by the disinterested friendship of Pickersgill. Two or three were bought by my friend Mr Archdeacon Fisher – from affection, being my schoolfellow – and two or three have found a home in France, bought of me by a dealer at a hundred guineas each, one of which was sold in Paris for four hundred guineas. The others are still mine. I have never yet had the good fortune to see the face of an English patron of art.

Do not, my dear Phillips, believe for a moment that I speak thus in the spirit of complaint. My ambition has been to form, if possible, an original feature of English landscape, and to do any little good in my power to that institution that has so far honoured me, and for which I am grateful, and for my education.

To endeavour to do this, however, I have sacrificed the best part of my life and not a little of paternal property. I am now past the age of fifty, Mrs Constable has most delicate health, and has seven infant children who have to look to me for everything in this world.

I don't feel uncomfortable while I am writing this sad letter to you, because I have long known you to be a man whose whole conduct is governed by the highest principles of probity and honour. And my object in writing to you at all is that I may be placed in your mind – fairly – in the list of my worthy brother candidates. I know I possess your esteem, of which I am proud, and am anxious at one time or other to receive your support, which I have never yet been fortunate enough to obtain.
I am, my dear Sir, Yrs very sincerely, John Constable.

Thompson scores a success

Elizabeth Thompson, better known under her married name of Lady Butler, had exhibited at the Royal Academy before 1874. However, in that year she showed 'The Roll Call'.

This delighted letter to her father describes the picture's reception at the private view. The competition for the painting was fierce, for although it had been bought by a Manchester collector, the Prince of Wales wanted it; the question was regally resolved by Queen Victoria who bought it herself.

(to her father)[5] May 1, 1874

Dearest – –,

I feel as though I were undertaking a really difficult work in attempting to describe to you the events of this most memorable day. I don't suppose I ever can have another such day, because, however great my future successes may be, they can never partake of the character of this one. It is my first great success. As Tom Taylor told me today, I have suddenly burst into flame, and this *first time* can never come home again. It has a character peculiar to all *first things* and to them alone. You know that 'the *elite* of London society' goes to the Private View. Well, the greater part of the *elite* have been presented to me this day, all with the same hearty words of congratulations on their lips and the same warm shake of the hand ready to follow the introductory bow. I was not at all disconcerted by all these bigwigs. The Duke of Westminster invited me to come and see the pictures at Grosvenor House, and the old Duchess of Beaufort was so delighted with 'The Roll Call' that she asked me to tell her the history of each soldier, which I did, the knot of people which, bye the bye, is always before the picture swelling into a little crowd to see me and, if possible, catch what I was saying. Galloway's tall figure was almost a fixture near the painting. That poor man, he was sadly distracted about this Prince of Wales affair, but the last I heard from him was that he *couldn't* part with it.

Some one at the Academy offered him £1000 for it, and T. Agnew told him that he would give anything he asked, but he refused those offers without a moment's hesitation. He has telegraphed to his wife at Manchester, as he says women can decide so much better than men on the spur of the moment. The Prince gives him till dinner tomorrow to make up his mind . . . Col Lloyd Lindsay, of Alma fame, and his wife were wild to have 'The Roll Call.' She shyly told me she had cried before the picture. But, for enthusiasm, William Agnew beat them all. He came up to be introduced, and spoke in such expressions of admiration that his voice positively shook, and he said that, having missed purchasing this work he would feel 'proud and happy' if I would paint him one, the time, subject and price, whatever it might be, being left entirely to me. Sir Richard Airey, the man who wrote the fatally misconstrued order on his holster and handed it to Nolan on the 25th October, 1854, was very cordial, and showed that he took a keen interest in the picture. I told him I valued a Crimean man's praise more than anybody else's, and I repeated the observation later to old Sir William Codrington under similar circumstances, and to other Crimean officers. One of them, whose father was killed at the assault on the Redan, pressed me very hard to consent to paint him two Crimean subjects, but I cannot promise anything more till I have worked out my already too numerous commissions, old ones, at the horrible old prices . . .

Millais is apprehensive

In 1859 Millais was at a critical point in his career. Early success had given way to public uncertainty about his work. Ruskin, whose former wife Millais had married in 1855, was antagonistic, and there was other press criticism; the dealers were doubtful of their profits in buying his work. His letters begin with a fit of unease.

(to his wife)[6] April 28th, 1859

I got home here last night after a hard day's rubbing at the pictures, which improved them immensely. I see things are creeping favourably on. Landseer this year is a most energetic admirer; he said yesterday, before many of the members, that my pictures are beyond everything I have ever done. Roberts, too, said I was sure to sell them at the private view. I have a few truly good friends [?] in the Royal Academy, *among the best men*, in spite of the wicked clique who, of course, do their best to run me down. There is no great 'catch' this year, except perhaps Orchard's [?] companion picture to his last year's one. It is very good (well painted) but egregiously vulgar and commonplace; but there is enough in it of a certain 'jingo' style to make it a favourite. This work may at first attract, but after a while it will not stand with the public.

Ruskin will be disgusted this year, for all the rubbish he had been praising *before being sent into the Royal Academy* has now bad places. There is a wretched work like a photograph of some place in Switzerland, evidently painted under his guidance, for he seems to have lauded it up sky-high: and that is *just where it is* in the miniature room! He does not understand my work, which is now too broad for him to appreciate, and I think his eye is only fit to judge the portraits of insects. But then, I think he has lost all real influence as a critic.

Tomorrow is the private view. I have given my tickets to John Leech and his wife. He knows all the press men, *and is respected by all*, so his opinions will be taken and carry weight. . . .

The next day things had not improved.

(to his wife) April 29th

I have just come from the private view. To tell you the truth, I think it is likely that I shall not sell one of the pictures. The clique has been most successful against me this year, and few people look at my work. Ruskin was there, looking at 'The Nuns'; and Tom Taylor, who said nothing. Everywhere I hear of the infamous attempts to destroy me (the truth is these pictures are not vulgar enough for general appreciation). However, I must wait, for I don't know what the Press will say yet. Seeing that there is a strong current against me, it is possible they may lift me up.

Gambart was there, and several dealers, *but none spoke to me*. They are not anxious to *look into my eyes just now*, and no wonder! Reade is sitting beside me as I write this.

The fact of the matter is, I am out of fashion. There will doubtless be a reaction, but the state of affairs in the Art world is at present too critical to admit of a good reward for all my labour. This is rather trying to me, I confess, after all my slavery, but it will account to you for my want of belief in the profession. You see, nobody knows anything about Art, so one is all at sea. The failures are most terrible in London just now, and things look very bad. What will become of Art, I don't know. It will not be worth following, if I cannot sell pictures such as these. I am sorry I have no good news for you, dear, but the outlook is anything but refreshing.

But then the artist had a spurt of hope, although remaining rather despondent about his chances of sales.

(to his wife) May 13th

There is a decided improvement in the look of things. Gambart writes me a long letter, and I have a commission for a picture from New York. I am perfectly certain that there will be a reaction in my favour, sooner or later, as the abuse has been so violent. I wish I could afford to keep the pictures, as I am perfectly sure they will one day fetch very large sums. There is no chance of my selling my pictures to *gentlemen* – the dealers are too strong. Picture-buyers can barter with them when they cannot with the artist, and my pictures have remained unsold so long that no one will believe they are valuable. All the other pictures of any pretensions in the exhibition are sold. This is, of course, fearfully dispiriting and a matter of wonder to me, as I have a high reputation; but my detractors have really induced the public to believe that the faults in my pictures spoil all the beauties. The crowds, too, round the pictures increase, but I am too disgusted to think more about them. If I sell them, I will wipe the memory of them for ever from my mind, they have been such torments to me.

In fact, the picture dealers came round, and 'The Vale of Rest' called here 'The Nuns', Millais's major exhibit was sold. On 17 May the artist was able to write:

I now have enough commissions to last me all next year, so I am quite happy. I am so glad to hear you are getting well and strong again. That is better than all the sales of pictures.

Renoir's exhibition policy

Towards the end of the century the question of where painters and sculptors should exhibit was far from straightforward. Both in London and Paris there were alternatives to the official shows, while in Vienna the name of the *Sezession* blazoned that group's opposition status. Some artists refused as a matter of principle to show at the Royal Academy or the Salon. Pierre Auguste Renoir, despite his part in the group activities of the Impressionists, took a more pragmatic line. We can follow his argument in the following letter to his dealer Durand-Ruel.

(to Paul Durand-Ruel)[7] Algiers, March 1881

My dear Monsieur Durand-Ruel,
I have just been trying to explain to you why I sent pictures to the Salon. In Paris there are scarcely fifteen people capable of liking a painter who doesn't show at the Salon. There are 80,000 who won't buy so much as a nose from a painter who is not hung at the Salon. That's why I send in two portraits a year, little as that is. Besides, I do not want to fall in with the mania for believing a thing is bad because of where it happens to be. In short, I don't want to waste time cherishing grudges against the Salon. I don't even want to seem to do so. In my opinion one should paint as well as possible, and that is all. Ah! If I were accused of neglecting my art, or sacrificing my opinions to idiotic ambition, I would understand my critics. But as that is not so, there is nothing they can reproach me with; on the contrary. At this moment, as always, I am concerned solely with doing good work. I want to paint stunning pictures you can sell for very high prices. I shall manage it before long, I hope. I have been keeping away from all other painters, in the sun, to think things out. I believe I have come to an end and found what I wanted. I may be wrong, but it would very much surprise me. Be patient for a little longer, and I hope I shall prove to you that one can show at the Salon and still do good painting.

So please plead my cause with my friends. I send to the Salon for purely commercial reasons. Anyhow, it's like with certain medicines. If it does no good, it does no harm.

I think I'm quite fit again now. I'm hoping to be able to work hard and make up for lost time.

At which point I wish you excellent health. And a lot of rich collectors. But keep them till I get back. I shall stay here another month. I don't want to leave Algiers without bringing back something from this marvellous country.

A thousand greetings to my friends and to you, Renoir.

The Council dines

As a footnote to the customs of the Academies, here is a comment from the turn of the century. The writer is Edwin Austin Abbey, an American newly elected as a Royal Academician on the strength of his historical painting.

(to his brother Will Abbey)[8] November 1899

On the last night of the year the outgoing Council dines the incoming Council in gorgeous fashion at the Academy, and as the old part of Burlington House is really very handsome – really magnificent, part of it, built in the early part of the last century – and it has been the custom since Sir Joshua's time for each new member upon his election to full honours to present a piece of plate to the Academy you can imagine the display is rather handsome. Years ago I bought a large silver meat skewer that had been Sir Joshua's property and had his coat of arms upon it. . . . I shall give that. The work in connection with the Academy is rather heavy for me for the next two years – a Council meeting once a week all the spring and winter, and once a month all the autumn, and six weeks solid on the Judging and Hanging Committees. With 13,000 pictures sent in, and barely room for 1,500, although 2000 are hung – it is no joke. I am also supposed to put on knee breeches and a shad-belly coat and go to a levee, but of this anon. . . .

Outside official shows

Lawrence tries to help Turner

The main public exhibitions through the century were supplemented by individual shows. Turner, as this letter documents, made up an exhibition of his own work in 1809; some years later, after Benjamin West's death in 1820 his sons set up a gallery in which their father's work was displayed. Later on, independent exhibitions by Manet and Courbet fell into this pattern. The friendly gesture by Lawrence to his young colleague was not successful, alas.

(to Mr Penrice of Yarmouth)[9] Greek Street, April 29th, 1809

Dear sir,
While you are meditating on the purchase of pictures of the Old Masters, what say you to setting an example to your rich friends of patronage to living artists? I have just been at the gallery of Mr Turner (indisputably the first landscape painter in Europe) and there seen a most beautiful picture which in my opinion would be very cheaply purchased at two hundred guineas – the price at which I understand it may be bought. The subject is *A Scene near Windsor*, with young Etonians introduced –

> Say, Father Thomas, for thou hast seen
> Full many a sprightly race, etc.

If the expression can apply to landscape it is full of sentiment, and certainly of genius. If you dare hazard the experiment you must do it quickly and authorize me to secure it for you. It would give me very great pleasure, from my respect for the powers of the artist, my admiration of the work, and (may I say it on so slight an acquaintance?) my esteem for you.

The size of the picture is (by guess) about three feet in length and a little less in height. It is his own peculiar manner, but *that* at its best; no Flemish finishing, but having it in fine principles of art, the essential of beauty, and (as far as the subject admits it) even of grandeur.

I remain, Dear Sir,
Very truly yours,

Thos. Lawrence.

Haydon sells a picture to the King

Benjamin Haydon was another artist who chose to set up a private exhibition of his work, in 1828. The show received a good deal of publicity, and also had a satisfactory outcome in a purchase by George IV.

Mary Russell Mitford, author of *Our Village*, was a life-long friend of the artist, and it was to her that Haydon tells his story.

(to Miss Mitford)[10] 23rd April, 1828

The King was sitting with an old friend of mine, and in talking of Art, asked him if he had 'seen Haydon's "Mock Election?" ' My friend replied he had. The King said, 'Would it please me if I saw it?' My friend said, 'I feel quite sure that your Majesty would be pleased.' The King then said, 'Will you get it for me to look at?' It was finally arranged that I should be asked if I had any objection to shut up the exhibition for a day, and if not, whether I would send the picture to the palace for one day. It was put to me with great delicacy – as a favour. I replied, 'For a day – for a month if the King likes.' It was then arranged that the picture should be sent the next morning to St James's Palace. When I came down to the exhibition at 10 a.m. the next morning, nothing was done. The picture was not moved, and there was only half-an-hour to get it down to the palace. I wrote all the names of the characters, with a particular or two of each of the catalogue, and took my leave after seeing the picture safe in the state apartments. At 2 p.m. I met Mr Seguier by appointment in the exhibition room. He took me aside. 'Well?' said I. 'Well,' said he. 'I congratulate you; the King is delighted, I never saw him more so. He said, "I hope Mr Haydon will let me have the picture today?" "Mr Haydon will leave it with your Majesty as long as you are pleased to keep it." Now,' said my friend, '*can* the King have it directly?' 'Certainly.' I said. 'Then meet me at twelve on Monday:' and we parted. The exhibition room was very full, and the ladies and gentlemen crowded about me and said, 'Oh, Mr Haydon, I have been coming this month, and now I shall never see it!' 'It shows very little regard for the King to take it away,' said another. 'It's a great shame,' said an angry gentleman. But the picture had been on exhibition three months and they had not come, and now they affected disappointment. Phipps, Lord Mulgrave's brother, went down to the palace the next day to see what had been done. He met Mr Seguier, and asked him. 'I'll tell you what has been done,' he said. 'I have five hundred guineas in my pocket for Haydon'; and on Monday at twelve I wrote: 'Received of his Majesty, five hundred guineas. B. R. Haydon.'

La Thierri dined with me; and we drank the King's health in the large goblet I had painted in his picture. God save the King!

Ever yours, B. R. Haydon.

Millet explains three pictures

All exhibitions had their critics, through whom the art on display became more widely known. The role of the critic has been extensively canvassed by historians, partly because published accounts are useful source material for them; what critics wrote, however, was not always informed by knowledge of what the artists intended. Alfred Sensier was a friend of Jean-François Millet, and wrote his criticism after having consulted the artist about his work. Millet was helpful, as this patient second reply to enquiries about three pictures demonstrates. Millet felt at some distance removed from interpretations of his work. Indeed, he wrote three years later to the same correspondent: 'My critics are, I suppose, men of learning and taste; but I cannot put myself into their shoes, and as all my life I have seen nothing but fields, I do my best to tell what I saw and felt when I was working there. There is plenty of opportunity for those who would like to do better, of course'.[11]

The pictures about which Millet writes were on show at a dealer's gallery.

(to Sensier)[11] 1860

My dear Sensier,

This is more or less what I wrote to Thoré about three of my pictures at Martinet's:

In 'Woman who has just been drawing Water', I tried to show a woman who is not a water-carrier, nor even a servant, but who had just been drawing water for use in her own house, water to make soup for her husband and children; who should not seem to be carrying either more or less than the weight of the full buckets; I wanted her face to wear an expression of rustic kindliness, showing through the sort of grimace imposed upon it, as it were, by the weight dragging at her arms and the light that makes her screw up her eyes. I avoided, as usual, with a kind of horror, any suggestion of sentimentality. On the contrary, I wanted to show her occupied – with simplicity and good humour, not looking on it as a burden – in something which, like the other household tasks, is part of her day's work, the habit of a lifetime. I wanted also to convey an idea of the coolness of the well and to show, by its antique appearance, that many women before this one must have come to draw water from it.

In 'Woman Giving her Children a Meal', I wanted to suggest the idea of a brood of fledgelings being fed by their mother in the nest. The man goes to work to feed these creatures.

In 'Sheep being sheared', I tried to express the kind of bewilderment and confusion that sheep feel when their thick wool has just been cut off, and the curiosity and stupefaction of those that have not been sheared, when their naked companions come back among them. I tried to make the place look like a peaceful, rustic dwelling, so that one can imagine the little field that lies behind it, and the poplars planted there to provide shade; in short to give it a long-standing air that calls forth memories.

I also told him, in case he might think it worth mentioning, that I try to make things look not as though they had been brought together pell-mell and for the occasion, but as though there were some indispensable, inevitable bond between them.

I would like the beings I depict to look as though they were pledged to their condition so that one cannot imagine it could occur to them to be anything different. People and objects must always be there for some purpose. I want to show lavishly and emphatically all that is necessary, for in my opinion things said feebly would be almost better left unsaid, because in that way they are somehow violated and spoilt, but I have the greatest horror of superfluities (however brilliant) and of padding, which can only distract the eye and weaken the effect.

I don't know whether all that was worth saying, but that was how it went. Tell me what you think. Will you come on Saturday, as you seemed almost to have decided? No news here. The children's whooping-cough seems to be calming down a little.

The family send you their greetings.

Pissarro on Whistler and picture hanging

In the first letter here Pissarro comments on the reputation of Whistler both as an artist and as an installer of exhibitions.

(to Lucien Pissarro)[12] Osny, February 28, 1885

My dear son,

So now you are going to wear tails for the first time. It is a good thing you have the clothes. You will have embarrassments enough in an entirely new milieu, with strange customs and ways of behaviour. What wonderful things to observe.

How I regret not having seen the Whistler show; I would have liked to have been there so much for the fine dry points as for the setting, which for Whistler has so much importance; he is even a bit too *pretentious* for me, aside from this I should say that for the room white and yellow is a charming combination. The fact is that we ourselves made the first experiments with colors: the room in which I showed was lilac, bordered with canary yellow. But we poor little rejected painters lack the means to carry out our concepts of decoration. As for urging Durand-Ruel to hold our exhibition in a hall decorated by us, it would, I think, be wasted breath. You saw how I fought with him for white frames, and finally I had to abandon the idea. No! I do not think that Durand-Ruel can be won over.

Whistler makes drypoints mostly, and sometimes regular etchings, but the suppleness you find in them, the pithiness and delicacy which charm you derive from the inking which is done by Whistler himself; no professional printer could substitute for him, for inking is an art in itself and completes the etched line. Now we would like to achieve suppleness *before* the printing. I saw two prints exhibited in Paris a year or two ago: they were rather delicate, meager and thin looking, one would have to see a whole collection in order to judge them, for doubtless he has done some that are first rate.

I reread your postscript on aesthetics. I wouldn't want to be an aesthete, at least like those across the Channel. *Aestheticism* is a kind of romanticism more or less combined with trickery, it means breaking for oneself a crooked road. They would have liked to make something like that out of impressionism, which really should be nothing more than a theory of observation, without entailing the loss of fantasy, freedom, grandeur, all that makes for great art. But not *eccentricity* to make people swoon.

Painters often felt badly about how their pictures were displayed. In large exhibitions the desired position was at eye level, known as the line. Because of the large number of paintings accepted, the whole wall was used, leaving paintings near the ceiling skyed. The same problems did not extend to dealers' galleries, where fewer works were shown, but as Pissarro complains in his letter to his son, the work of a painter showing with others could be disadvantaged.

Paris (May 15, 1887)

My dear Lucien,
I shall do my best to leave by the beginning of the week. I would have liked to see you here in Paris, to get your reaction to the Millet show, to ours, and to mine especially. I wanted to send you a little money, I made every effort to, I have only been able to borrow forty francs from Heymann; I must carefully husband part of this money so as to be able to return to Paris if need be. Heymann's collectors lost heavily during the recent crises, some time will have to elapse before they regain confidence.

You must remember that Heymann recruits his collectors from the small capitalists. – This is very distressing since I can count only on people of that sort.

Petit has undertaken to push Monet and Sisley, hence it hardly matters to him whether or not I get anywhere; he has his faithful collectors who recruit buyers here and there. I observed these gentlemen several times propagandizing exclusively for Monet and Sisley. The placement of pictures was done in advance, the grouping was calculated, I know that; talking with Sisley I got what practically amounts to an admission. So you see my canvases were scattered to give them less importance. I let them get away with it this year, I didn't want to say anything; besides I was afraid that my canvases would not show well with the others. This was unnecessary modesty on my part, grouped around my *Apple Eaters* (695), my show would have been much superior.

Yesterday I saw Bracquemond. He likes my large painting (695) less than my new things, he finds these last very excellently drawn and more pure and delicate in color; he did not even notice from where we were sitting, that they are *pointillist* works. I called this to his attention, he replied that this could not affect his judgement, that he would not take sides for or against. – On the other hand he finds the Sisleys first rate and the Monets beautiful. However he was rather critical of Renoir, though he thought some parts of the large painting very well drawn – I am of his opinion as to the parts. – It is the ensemble, the synthesis which is faulty, and this they refuse to understand! – He also noted the crude execution in some of the Monets, particularly in one of the Holland canvases, in which the impasto is so thick that an unnatural light is added to the canvas, you can hardly conceive how objectionable it is to me, – even worse is the swept and meager sky – no, I cannot accept this approach to art. – But the walls in the picture seem to me very well treated. As for Sisley, I just can't enjoy his work, it is commonplace, forced, disordered; Sisley has a good eye, and his work will certainly charm all those whose artistic sense is not very refined. – Madame Morisot is doing good work, she had neither advanced nor fallen back, she is a fine artist. Whistler is very artistic; he is a showman, but nevertheless an artist. These are my impressions. As for myself I have some doubts about my work – that is inevitable, but I feel that I have certainly made progress. I want to know how I can put this progress to account in figure compositions done in the studio. This is what I shall attempt next year. I need to do two large canvases and several landscapes. Will I have the peace of mind to carry out this venture successfully? I will do my best. Seurat, Signac, Fenéon, all our young friends, like only my works and Madame Morisot's a little; naturally they are motivated by our common struggle. But Seurat, who is colder, more logical and more moderate, does not hesitate for a moment to declare that we have the right position, and that the impressionists are even more retarded than before.

An Impressionist fiasco

Berthe Morisot's work was highly esteemed by her Impressionist friends. This is a thank you letter for compliments from Monet. The occasion was the last Impressionist exhibition to be held.

(to Monet)[13] 1886

Thank you very much for remembering me so kindly and for your words about my wretched paintings at Durand's. I am all the more touched because, as you know, the show is a complete fiasco, and it seems to me that all of us have had a share in the responsibility for this disaster. Renoir and Whistler of course less than the others. But all this is incomprehensible to the public at large.

As for you, you have conquered this recalcitrant public. At Goupil's one meets only people who have the highest admiration for your works, and I think you are playing the coquette in asking me for my opinion of them. In actual fact I am dazzled by them, a fact which you must know quite well. If you insist, however, the one I like best is the picture with the little reddish-brown tree in the foreground. My husband and I stood in ecstasy in front of it for an hour.

I saw Mallarmé on Thursday. I would not be surprised if this charming man is in the process of writing a letter to you to express his admiration of the exhibition. Both of us are still very eager to visit you at Giverny, and I hope that next month the weather will be less unpleasant than it is now. Give my best regards to Mme Hoschedé.

5
Portraits

The most reliable source of commissions for artists was portraiture. The range of people who wanted to be recorded grew with increased prosperity, so that others besides the well born and the famous commissioned portraits. Letters survive for all classes of portraiture, but perhaps there is a natural inclination for readers to be more interested in those which are about special sitters.

It was through portrait drawing that James Sharples earned his living in Pennsylvania during the last decade of the eighteenth century. His wife Ellen Sharples started out by copying her husband's work, but after his death she took to practising on her own account, first in America and then in England. Here is what she wrote:

> I had frequently thought that every well educated female, particularly those who only had small fortunes, should at least have the power, (even if they did not exercise it,) by the cultivation of some available talent, of obtaining the conveniences and some of the elegancies of life and be enabled to preserve that respectable position in society to which they had been accustomed. Many circumstances had led to the formation of this opinion, not only the French Revolution, which occasioned the entire loss of fortune to the great number of ladies and gentlemen who sought refuge in this and other countries. The reverse of fortune had been frequently observed in married and single ladies, a few the loss of their whole income, others of a part, obliging

> them to observe the strictest economy. In mercantile and various other concerns, men of abilities once affluent had become poor, others by thoughtlessness and extravagance. . . . The continual fluctuation of the funds and other property in which our money had been invested, the uncertainty in mechanical pursuits in which Mr. S. delighted – all had an influence in deciding me, soon after our arrival in Philadelphia where Congress was assembled, to make my drawing which had been learnt and practised as an ornamental art for amusement, available to a useful purpose. Mr. S. was generally engaged in drawing in crayons the portraits of the most distinguished Americans, foreign Ministers and other distinguished visitants from Europe. Copies were frequently required; these I undertook and was so far successful as to have as many commissions as I could execute; they were thought equal to the originals, price the same; we lived in good style associating with the first society.[1]

In short portrait drawing was a stand-by resorted to in the same way as teaching. There was a ready market. Miniatures were a little more elaborate than drawings, and required a special aptitude for delicate work. However, drawings, miniatures and paintings all played roles in social life, as possessions, records, and focuses of sentiment. Constable, for example, wrote to his fiancée about the portrait he had painted of her: 'I am sitting before your portrait – which when I look off the paper is so extremely like that I can hardly help going up to it. I never had an idea before of the real pleasure a portrait could afford.' And in another letter: 'I would not be without your portrait for the world. The sight of it calms my spirit under all the trouble and it is always the first thing I see in the morning and the last at night.'[2]

Gentle portraits of family and friends, paintings of acquaintances or run-of-the-mill portraits of tradespeople and minor gentry are often almost unrecorded. The same may be said for many portraits by painters with busy practices, whose sitters' books may be the only clue to the identity of a portrait. A uniform or a dress may be splendid and even informative, but the person may remain an enigma, and a letter to resolve such a puzzle is likely to be an unusual and lucky find. One of the few sorts of ordinary and informal portraits that may be identified is the artist's self-portrait.

The self-portrait is a fascinating category of art; while some self-portraits are unassuming, such as those destined for family ownership or intimates, a few artists have made their own pictures more revealing. Rembrandt's self-portraits are the subjects for several books, and in van Gogh we have a rare example of a self-portraitist who has also commented on his images of himself. Here is an extract from a letter to his brother Theo in 1888:

> So now at last I have a chance to compare my painting with what the comrades are doing. My portrait, which I am sending to Gauguin in exchange, holds its own, I am sure of that. I have written to Gauguin in reply to his letter that if I might be allowed to stress my own personality in a portrait, I had done so in trying to convey in my portrait not only myself but also an impressionist in general, had conceived it as the portrait of a Bonze, a simple worshipper of the eternal Buddha. And when I put Gauguin's conception and my own side by side, mine is as grave, but less despairing . . . Someday you will also see my self-portrait, which I am sending to Gauguin, because he will keep it, I hope. It is all ashen gray against pale malachite (no yellow). The clothes are this brown coat with a blue border, but I have exaggerated the brown into purple, and the width of the blue borders. The head is modeled in light colours painted in a thick impasto against the light background with hardly any shadows. Only I have made the eyes slightly slanting like the Japanese.[3]

Self-portraits did not, however, make an artist a profitable living. That was the reward of more mundane work, or the unusual opportunities of portraying the powerful or the famous. A Prime Minister like Gladstone qualified on both counts, as is documented by a letter from a portraitist commenting on a visit to Hawarden, Gladstone's country estate. Meanwhile we can look first at a letter to an artist describing the success of a friendly plot.

Distinguished people

A surprise party

We have already seen that Harriet Hosmer benefited from generous and timely support from Wayman Crow, who enabled her to continue her studies in Rome. She found an ingenious and delicate way to show her appreciation, some twelve years later, with the help of a friend in St Louis.

Washington University, St Louis, Missouri was founded by a grandfather of T. S. Eliot. Harriet Hosmer's friend describes a unique and splendid occasion there.

(to Harriet Hosmer from Mr J. E. Yeatman)[4] St Louis, June 19, 1868

My dear Miss Hosmer:

You may now write, 'Veni, Vidi, Vici'. The day has passed, the bust has been presented, all has gone well. Last evening the commencement exercises of the university took place, and the giving of the diplomas. There had been an alcove built on the platform, at the rear, lined with crimson brocade, in which the pedestal and bust had been placed with crimson curtains in front to conceal it. This created no suspicion, but was thought to be intended as a background for the chancellor's chair. The front seats were occupied by the president and members of the board of trustees, among whom was Mr Crow, and by the professors of the university. After the speaking was over and the diplomas had been delivered, the chancellor moved his chair to one side and drew aside the curtain revealing the bust. It was such a surprise that it was received with a burst of applause. When it ceased I arose and made the presentation. Mr Crow was the most surprised man of them all, and I may also say the most gratified. My remarks occupied less than five minutes, and I did not mention either your name or that of Mr Crow till the very last, when they were received with a round of long and loud cheers. The president, Dr Eliot, made an appropriate reply, accepting the gift in the name of the college, and giving its history and its arrival in this country entirely unknown to any one except to himself and to me. So you see your instructions have been carried out. The secrecy and non-formality added greatly to the interest of the occasion, and showed that you were an artist in other things than sculpture. There were many pleasant incidents connected with it. Dr Eliot referred to Mr Crow has having framed the wise and broad charter, and to his substantial donation, which was the initial one in founding the university. The likeness is considered perfect, and I must congratulate you upon its success in every way. I have written you thus in detail, as I know you will be waiting to hear. . . .

Very sincerely yours, James E. Yeatman

Holl helps to saw down a walnut tree

Frank Holl was delighted to be invited to paint Gladstone; he quickly decided that he should be portrayed standing, 'as I think a character like Mr Gladstone should be; to *sit* is to be at ease, and not the character of the at once wonderful and extraordinary life he has led.'

The sittings went well, and in the following letter Holl reports on his progress, including his joining in with Gladstone's well-known recreation, cutting down trees.

(to his wife)[5]

Even now I feel it quite difficult to say whether for certain I return Saturday. I must leave it open. If I can, I shall do so, although I am most perfectly delighted with my visit. Mr Gladstone is, I can quite see, *all with me*, and Agnew (who arrived about an hour ago) tells me that Mr Gladstone followed him into his room and said, 'I have been painted before, but never have I enjoyed an experience like this; your young friend is so mightily in earnest, I can't help standing to him: I feel *part* of it!' Lords Spencer and Granville, who arrived last evening, are in no way in the way; our sitting today went on as usual, and this afternoon I have been with Mr Gladstone and his son, W. H., and brought down a very large walnut tree, at which we have been cutting the last three evenings, between the lights. On the whole, my visit is one to be remembered for its pleasures. With regard to the portrait remains to be seen. Of course I must have my studio to work on it, and I shall bring it home in a state of unfinish (excepting the head) . . .

This letter encourages the inclusion of a brief complementary entry from the artist's diary.

Mrs Gladstone picked up some chips, carrying away an armful; she said, 'They make very good *letter weights*' – Why not? the world is very hard, and only too ready to throw stones. Mr Gladstone never cuts trees unless they are really dying or rotting away (this walnut tree had a large rot eating into its root), or else trees that are too close together; and for exercise, for he is quite fond of this kind of exercise (though I doubt the advisability of such hard labour at his time of life). Then if the world of his admirers are anxious and desirous of having mementoes of their admired chief, why should not these chips be sold? (already they have an enormous number of applications); and what would it be if they were to be had for the asking?

An amiable squabble

A friendly arrangement for a portrait by Daniel Maclise brought a cheque from Charles Dickens; but the painter would have none of it. Equally, Dickens did not want to be denied.

(to Charles Dickens)[6]

My dear Dickens, How could *you* think of sending me a cheque for what was to me a matter of gratification? I am almost inclined to be offended with you. May I not be permitted to give some proof of the value I attach to your friendship? I return the cheque, and regret that you should have thought it necessary to send it to yours faithfully, Daniel Maclise.

(to Daniel Maclise)

Do not be offended. I quite appreciate the feeling which induced you to return what I sent you; notwithstanding, I *must* ask you to take it back again. If I could have contemplated for an instant the selfish engrossment of so much of your time and extraordinary powers, I should have had no need (knowing you, I knew that well) to resort to the little device I played off.

I will take anything else from you at any time that you will give me, any scrap from your hand; but I entreat you not to disturb this matter. I am willing to be your debtor for anything else in the whole wide range of your art, as you shall very readily find whenever you put me to the proof.

A tableau by Whistler

Count Robert de Montesquiou, a source for Proust's character of the Baron de Charlus in *A la Recherche du Temps Perdu* was painted to his great satisfaction by Whistler. The painter wrote to his wife describing a viewing of the portrait by the Count himself and Madame de Montebello; in this extract they are pinned down on his paper like rare butterflies.

(to his wife)[7]

He is enchanted! – and this evening he went upstairs and brought down Madame de Montebello, who was standing for her picture to Gandara, poor fellow – I was not displeased that he should do so, for the whole picture had not yet sunk in – and the background and the figure all went beautifully together – Chinkie I wish you could have seen the two in front of the work! They were splendid! These two amazing ones – all 'respectueux' and absolutely without a doubt! – a sort of unveiling in Olympus – or last tableau in a very superior pantomime! Montesquiou was of course simply heroic – 'triste et noble' – and childlike in his joy – It was really without precedent – in my experience – for *expression* of such sympathy is unknown to me hitherto – and impossible in England – Not that there was anything loud or accentuated even in their demonstration but they gloried in the picture – as an apotheosis of themselves, their birth, their 'race'! 'It is the acme of pride', said the Count, 'untainted with vanity'!! 'C'est noble' said the grande dame with a sort of religious intonation – and there they were really worshipping before a sort of *monument* of their blue blood! – Well you know Chinkie no more intoxicating recognition could possibly be offered the Wams than such appreciation as this – I dare scarcely believe that the picture can be as superbe as in the gloaming it looked – You know how the poor grinder is lonely and timid in the morning – and how he lives in terror of the first peep at his painting before breakfast – meanwhile however there is no doubt that Madame de Montebello looked at the portrait in its highest sense of achievement – no little thoughts of detail – no wishing for more of this or less of that – simply a supreme acceptation of the whole as the highest possible incarnation of all that is beautiful and dignified and magnificent – 'C'est Splendide!' she told Gandara when she went back to that sad Spaniard – un chef d'oeuvre! and certainly in the flattering light of the evening our Montesquiou poete et grande seigneur did look stupendous – Bunnie I believe would never have forgiven him – and William's 'Lofty' was a pale expression for him. But *more Obi* Chinkie that I may not think ill of him tomorrow! . . .

Royal portraits

Lawrence and Princess Charlotte

Lawrence's outstanding reputation as a portrait painter was fostered by the success of many Royal commissions. One of these proved the occasion for two memorable letters to his close friend, Mrs Wolff.

His sitter was Princess Charlotte, the daughter of the Prince Regent and his estranged wife. The Princess had married Prince Leopold, later King of the Belgians.

(to Mrs Wolff)[8]

I am now returned from Claremont, my visit to which was agreeable to me in every respect; both in what regarded myself, my reception, and the complete success of my professional labours, and in the satisfaction of seeing the perfect harmony in which this young couple now live, and of observing the good qualities which promise to make it lasting.

The princess is, as you know, wanting in elegance of deportment, but has nothing of the hoyden or of the boisterous hilarity which has been ascribed to her; her manner is exceedingly frank and simple, but not rudely abrupt or coarse; and I have, in this little residence of nine days, witnessed undeniable evidence of an honest, just, English nature, that reminded me, from its immediate decision between the right and wrong of a subject, and the downrightness of the feeling that governed it, of the good King, her grandfather . . .

Their mode of life is very regular: they breakfast together alone about eleven: at half-past twelve she came in to sit to me, accompanied by Prince Leopold, who stayed a great part of the time: about three she would leave the painting room to take her airing round the grounds in a low phaeton with her ponies, the Prince always walking by her side: at five she would come in and sit to me till seven: at six or before it he would go out with his gun to shoot either hares or rabbits, and return about seven or half-past: soon after which we went to dinner, the Prince and Princess appearing in the drawing-room just as it was served up. Soon after the dessert appeared, the Prince and Princess retired to the drawing-room, whence we soon heard the pianoforte accompanying their voices . . . After coffee, the card-table was brought, and they sat down to whist, the young couple being always partners, the others changing. You know *my superiority* at whist, and the unfairness of my sitting down with unskilful players; I therefore did not obey the command, and from ignorance of the delicacy of my motives, am recommended to study Hoyle before my second visit there next week, which indeed must be a very short one.

Alas, the Princess died in childbirth. Lawrence recorded the sequel as follows.

(to Mrs Wolff)

I was at Claremont on a call of enquiry the Saturday before her death. Her last command to me was, that I should bring down the picture to give to Prince Leopold upon his birthday, the 16th of the next month.

It was my wish that Prince Leopold should see the picture on his first entering the room to his breakfast, and accordingly at seven o'clock I set off with it in a coach. I got to Claremont, uncovered and placed it in the room in good time. Before I took it there, I carried it in to Colonel Addenbroke, Baron Hardenbroch, and Dr. Short who had been her tutor. Dr. Short looked at it for some time in silence, but I saw his lips trembling, and his eyes filled to overflowing. He said nothing, but went out; and soon after him Colonel Addenbroke. The Baron and I then placed the picture in the Prince's room.

When I returned to take my breakfast, Colonel Addenbroke came in: he said, 'I don't know what to make of these fellows; there's Sir Robert Gardiner swears he can't stay in the room with it; that if he sees it in one room he'll go into another' . . . As I passed through the hall Dr. Short came up to me (he had evidently been, and was crying) and thanked me for having painted such a picture. 'No one is a better judge than I am, Sir,' and he turned away . . . The Prince was looking exceedingly pale; but he received me with calm firmness, and that low, subdued voice that you know to be the *effort* at composure. He spoke at once about the picture and of its value to him more than the world besides. From the beginning to the end of the interview he was greatly affected. He checked his first burst of affection by adverting to the public loss and that of the Royal family. 'Two generations gone! – gone in a moment! I have felt for myself, but I have felt for the Prince Regent. My Charlotte has gone from this country – it has lost her. She was a good, she was an admirable woman. None could know my Charlotte as I did know her. It was my happiness, my duty to know her character, but it was my delight' . . .

The Tzar Alexander

Lawrence's most important commission was to paint for the Prince Regent the portraits of the leaders of the successful alliance against Napoleon. Two of his sitters in Vienna were Emperor Alexander of Russia, and Emperor Francis of Austria. The place and date was Aix-la-Chapelle in 1818. Lawrence here describes the first sitting of the Russian Emperor.

(to Mrs Wolff)

He came entirely alone but full-dress'd. As he passed through the Hall he said, taking me by the Arm or rather by the Wrist – 'I am afraid I have made you wait. The King of Prussia came to me and kept me.'

As he went up Stairs He said, 'How do you do today. I hope you keep well. Are you not fatig'd yourself with Business?' . . .

He then asked if he should now sit, would not suffer me to take his hat, but went to a Chair at some distance to put it down. Soon after he had seated himself Genl Ouvaroff in plain Clothes came in.

His I.M. sat again remarkably well and I finally succeeded; but certainly I have less and less confidence as I grow old. The waiting and the suspense is a nervous thing. The going up and coming down the Stairs unsettles one, and the first quarter of an hour in agitation and doubt spite of all previous determination. But Mrs. Siddons said she could never yet face an Audience without something of apprehension, and I must therefore be well content to endure this Weakness.

I have been quite as successful as in the dear Emperor Francis. He keeps all in awe, but he is still I see greatly belov'd by all his Officers.

His Aide de Camps, fine young men, quite dance about the Picture, mad with Joy at its being so like him. The Figure is not sketch'd in, and they put themselves into Postures to shew me how he stands, not gracefully (as they say), but he stands so . . .

He sat admirably, keeping his Head and very frequently his Eye in the exact direction that I pointed out, but all the while, except in short answers or questions to me, engag'd in very animated Conversation with his attendant Genl Ouvaroff in Russ. . . .

You know how long it is before one gets under weigh in Painting – before the Pencil can mould the Color into shape, before that shape has *general* accuracy of form, before truth of Hue and Tone is united to it, and then the fleeting moment of Expression given. These were golden minutes to me, and I happily succeeded; whilst the Emperor seem'd to forget the time in mixd indulgence to me, and enthusiasm on his subject. I should have certainly held him longer, but that the Ministers crept in on Tip-toe from the Conferences and terminated the Sitting.

They all gave their approbation to my Work – the Emperor himself looked attentively at it, not displeasingly, then appointed to come at the same hour tomorrow; and on leaving me quietly and firmly took me by the Hand . . .

An equestrian speculation

Thomas Thornycroft was responsible for an equestrian statue of Queen Victoria at the Great Exhibition of 1851. There are luckily several letters from the artist about his work. The first is about a visit made by Prince Albert to the sculptor's studio.

(to W B Dickinson)[9] March 14, 1851

His interest was not expressed in a few empty expressions of admiration, but was sustained in an earnest examination of the design and mode of treatment which occupied a full hour and a quarter, and even then he was driven away by the approach of night. We had a famous talk, the excitement enabling me to say much in a few words. Every part of the arrangement was canvassed. I am sadly pushed for time. Twelve months was necessary to finish such a work. It must go to the exhibition finished or unfinished or H.R.H. will be disappointed. To finish it is impossible, and I dread lest the work which impressed him as a bold and graceful design in the light of my own studio, will in the open air light of Crystal Palace disappoint him by its want of finish.

I have heard today that the Prince told his riding master after having seen the model, that he would have it in bronze. I tremble lest anything should thwart this commission. Everything hangs by it. The Prince's order to execute this life size in metal would ensure to me a public statue of colossal size.

My fortune vibrates in the balance. Success seems to dawn upon me when with hope deferred and straightened means I had almost despaired.

The statue was placed as the first work of sculpture seen by visitors to the Crystal Palace, and was well liked. It did not win a first class medal, which went to Marocchetti's statue of 'Richard Coeur de Lion', placed outside the entrance. Nevertheless, 'the iron Duke of Waterloo softened with pleasure at the sight of his Royal Mistress on her Charger', and the Queen was pleased.

18th April, 1851

The Queen herself has seen my group since I wrote to you. I was present but kept in the background the more securely to watch the impression made by my work. That she was gratified was evident enough. As she surveyed the statue she drew in her chin and closed firmly her mouth appreciating and identifying the character which I have aimed at in my impersonation of Her Majesty. Some words passed between the Queen and her Royal Consort regarding the work and her features relaxed into an unaffected smile of gratification and pleasure.

The Times is upon me again this morning. If today's abuse brings to me as many private expressions of approval as the first one produced, I shall grow weary of acknowledging compliments. The only sculpture worth(y) of *The Times* commendation is a grotesque pigmy 'Puck'!

Thornycroft was disappointed in his hope of having his statue commissioned as a bronze by the Prince Consort, but decided to publish it as a statuette, substituting for the crown 'a gay little feathered hat the Queen had worn when reviewing her troops at Chobham'. He showed the model to the royal couple at Windsor Castle; the Queen's instructions for Mary Thornycroft here mentioned refer to the commission she had been given for portraits of the royal children. Princess Alice represented Spring in a sequence of the four seasons.

The Prince came immediately and carefully examining the work in every view, expressed his approval of the design. He suggested an improvement to which I assented, and taking a modelling tool, H.R.H. set to work; whilst thus employed the Queen appeared, and rest content I made obeisance inspired by loyalty to the Sovereign and gratitude to my patron.

The Royal sculptor paused in his work that H.M. might see the design. As she passed round I saw her eyes meet those of her Royal Consort for a moment: 'It is good' was the Prince's reply to the silent enquiry.

'Yes, it is very good, I am sure it is', said the Queen, with that decision and emphasis that characterises her.

I shall not forget that moment: it was not alone the Queen's approval but it was the sincerity and truthfulness of her manner of giving it. 'It is like and sits well and the horse is full of spirit', rejoined the Prince.

H.R.H. took up the modelling tool again and H.M. turned to speak with me. I stated that I had made the design for a public statue, knowing that such works would be required, but that my immediate intention was to publish it as a statuette in bronze. H.M. then gave me an opportunity of comparing my work with her features, giving me her commands to Mrs Thornycroft as she did so. Thus ended. I shall keep my eyes on the empty pedestal at Charing Cross, believing I shall set a statue there.

6

Projects Great and Small

Artists employed by the state or other official authorities could be well rewarded for their work, which had the added advantage of being publicly visible, say in a church, a town hall or an opera house. Political circumstances had much to do with the scope of commissions; then as today, a change of regime could create a programme of public works. The relative instability of French politics caused more than one programme to be undertaken, one of the most spectacular being the historical paintings commissioned by Louis-Philippe for the palace at Versailles; arguably the most successful artistic programme was the decoration by Delacroix of the Palais de Luxembourg. In Britain, a major opportunity for mural decoration was created by the rebuilding of the Houses of Parliament, while in Germany many different states created a climate of competition for patronage.

Nationalism was an engine of change through the century, so that themes of national history and the portraying of national heroes are found everywhere. Bronze statues are among the most obvious symbols of this trend, but hero worship also extended to various projects for historical Pantheons, on both sides of the Atlantic. The century was also an active period of church building, creating opportunities for decorations, sculpture and murals. France in the latter part of the century was a secular state, and this unexpectedly provided funds for church decorations, paid for by the government; Ingres and Delacroix were among the beneficiaries.

Commissions from private patrons were not so dominant a feature of the art market in the nineteenth century as they had been in the previous century. The exhibiting societies created a mart of ready-made works from which collectors could choose; nevertheless there were works which were required for particular rooms, or to fit into existing interior schemes. Occasionally, a patron with as firm a mind as the Duke of Wellington would settle on a theme, and require a picture. The latter occasion provides a good letter from the lucky artist receiving his commission.

Prints made up a different sort of market, especially steel engravings which sold in large numbers. Other sorts of reproduction which gave employment to artists included wood engraving, important for book illustrations and magazines, and lithography, the run away commercial success of the century.

Official commissions

Trumbull argues his case

Artists' letters on business are indispensable for historians, who are seeking to establish facts and dates. Relatively few of them have wide general interest, but of those few, letters about famous public works rank high. One major American commission was for the murals of the Capitol at Washington.

John Trumbull had an unmatchable qualification for the job, since he had himself been a participant in the events he was to record. The application was successful, and the results can still be seen.

(to Thomas Jefferson)[1] 26 December 1816

Twenty eight years have elapsed, since under the kind protection of your hospitable roof at Chaillot, I painted your portrait in my picture of the Declaration of Independence, the composition of which had been planned two years before in your Library. The long period of War and Tumult which succeeded, palsied and suspended my work, and threw me as you know into other pursuits . . . The Government of the U.S. are restoring to more than their original Splender, the Buildings devoted to national purposes at Washington, which were barbarously sacrificed to the Rage of War. I have thought this a proper opportunity to make my first application for public patronage, and to request to be employed in decorating the walls of these buildings with the paintings which have employed so many (years) of my life . . . The Memory of your kindness & of the interest which you formerly took in this work is too strongly in my memory, to suffer a doubt to intrude of your powerful protection at this time, – again, the work has been carried thus far by my own unaided exertions *and can be finished only by me*: further Artists may arise with far Superior Talents, but time has already withdrawn almost all their Models; and I who was one of the youngest Actors in the early scenes of the War, passed the Age of Sixty: – no time remains therefore for hesitation. Hoping that my application will meet your approbation, & support, & that you will honor me with an Answer addressed to me at Washington – Poste restante –

Haydon tries his powers of persuasion

Benjamin Haydon was a persistent advocate of historical records in art; unfortunately his hopes of work on these lines were often disappointed. In the following exchanges he is attempting to persuade Lord Palmerston to commemorate a diplomatic conference; he was not successful.

(to Lord Palmsterson)[2] 4th November, 1833.

Dear Lord Palmerston,

You have more than once, with characteristic kindness, hinted to me that I should paint the 'Conference' at the Foreign Office. I need hardly tell you how highly honoured I should feel to be entrusted with such a commission, and with what energy I should devote myself to its execution as soon as I have finished Lady Grey's picture.

Believe me, my dear Lord, Your faithful servant, B. R. Haydon.

(from Lord Palmerston) Broadlands, 10th November 1833

Dear Sir,

All matters in this world, great and small, turn on finance, and before I answer your note I should like to know what would be about the expense of such a picture of the 'Conference' as you suggest.

The members would be Talleyrand for France, Esterhazy and Wessemberg for Austria, Lieven and Matuszewich for Russia, Bülow for

Prussia, myself for England, Dedel for Holland, and Van de Weyer for Belgium.

I return to town to-morrow, so direct your answer to Stanhope Street.

Dear Sir, yours faithfully, Palmerston.

(to Lord Palmerston) London, 12th November, 1833.

My dear Lord,

I know your axiom to be too true. If the portraits are the full size of life, and full length, as there would be nine portraits the price would be eight hundred guineas. If half the size of life and yet full length, five hundred guineas. If the size of life, like some of Sir Joshua's groups, as far as the knees, five hundred guineas.

I love my art; I do all myself because I love it, and I never make a 'job' of a picture and hurry it over by the assistance of others.

You will do me the kindness to understand distinctly that I wish to meet your views, because I wish to paint the picture. I am, my dear Lord, your faithful servant, B. R. Haydon.

(from Lord Palmerston) 26th November, 1833.

My dear Sir,

I ought to have sooner answered your note of the 12th. I am much obliged to you for the explanation it contains and I will think the matter over between this and the spring, and if I should feel up to a 'Conference' I will let you hear from me again.

My dear Sir, yours very faithfully, Palmerston.

(to Lord Palmerston) London, 28th November 1833.

My dear Lord,

Permit me to thank you for your kind note. I shall pray heartily all the winter that you may be 'up to a Conference' in the spring.

In the meantime, would it not be prudent to secure, by a sketch, Talleyrand? He is old and may drop off all of a sudden. But I leave that to your Lordship's discretion.

Believe me, my dear Lord, faithfully yours, B. R. Haydon.

Delacroix seeks adequate payment

Eugène Delacroix was commissioned in 1833 to paint the *Salon du Roi* in the Chamber of Deputies, one of the major schemes for the French state which he carried out with eclat. The progress of the work was tortuous, and by December 1836 the artist felt impelled to ask for more money, no doubt especially because he had been personally responsible for paying the gilders.

(to the Minister of the Interior)[3]

Rues des Marais Saint
Germain, no 17.
27 December 1836

Dear Minister

The decoration of the *Salon du Roi* in the Chamber of Deputies was in its original form not as complicated as today, and for which I have been asked to get the best result for its various parts. In the original project, there were only the panels of the ceiling to paint and the sections which separated the windows. The long frieze formed by figures which are now above the arcades have been added. But, by their number and importance, they have doubled the work. In the first arrangement there was, under the soffits which supported the ceiling, a strip which gave only a meagre space, and which could only be filled with ornamental design. It can be seen that the arrangement had a heavy and ungraceful appearance, increased by the extreme poverty of four figures isolated on the ceiling. The destruction of the ceiling was considered and replacing it by another, where the painting would have more space and be more appropriate for the *Salon.*

I then asked, instead of this destruction and the subsequent renovation for only the suppression of the strip which weighed on the opening of doors and windows. This measure was taken with the agreement of the architect and approved by M Thiers, then Minister of Public Works. This eliminated the cost of reconstituting the ceiling, and there is no reason to regret the loss that the previous order would have occasioned. But, in this new plan, what was only an insignificant decoration has become for the painter the main feature of the work, since this frieze consists of not less than seventy figures more or less worked out.

I have to say that I find some satisfaction in making the decoration more complete to compensate for the time spent, which so greatly exceeds my plans and the requirements of the Ministry. However, I am requesting you, Minister, to be kind enough to consider if there is not cause to accord me a fee appropriate to the importance the work has acquired. I also take the liberty of informing you that the ornaments which accompany the figures have been carried out by professional decorators at considerable expense, which I have undertaken. All the gilding in the ornament has also been paid for in this way.

I calculate that the low estimate, which had been fixed at 35,000 francs when the work was more limited, became insufficient if one considers the time needed for the subsequent plan. It certainly is if one considers the fees which have been allowed to artists for similar work. I will instance among others the hemicyle of the *Ecole des Beaux Arts*, the separate commissions for the Madeleine, each of which was paid 25,000 francs, and several more.

I have the honour to be, with respect, Minister, your very humble and obedient servant, Eugène Delacroix.

Courbet in Munich

Gustave Courbet had a growing reputation by the late 1860s, making it worth his while to travel from France to Munich for an exhibition in which his work was included. He was awarded a decoration, and was popular with the younger generation of Germans.

A realist like Courbet was sure to dislike the classical and historical decorations in Munich, and is characteristically sardonic about the city's public sculpture. He is able to comment freely to this correspondent, his friend the critic Jules Castagnary.

(to Jules Castagnary)[4] Interlaken, Switzerland, November 20

My dear Castagnary:

I left Munich two weeks ago. You said to write you because you might come. I did not feel it was worth the trouble of such a long trip. You will find the German newspapers that refer to the exhibition at the Munich embassy on the rue de Berry, Champs Elysées. They are very nice and will give you whatever you want. Only two of us were named officers of the Order of St Michael by the artists: M. Corot and I. The other two, M. Cabanel and M. Doré were nominated, the first for the painting of 'Adam and Eve', commissioned by King Maximilian, the father of the one who is reigning at present (the king nominated Cabanel by his own authority); Doré was nominated by the 'officiality', which means, I think, by the ministry, for services rendered in sending over French paintings.

There is almost no good painting in Germany. They are all concerned with the negative qualities of art. One of the principal qualities (they look for) is perspective. They talk about it all day long. Another important quality is the accuracy of historical costumes. They are very much into anecdotal painting, and all the walls in Munich are covered with frescoes as if they were wallpaper: red, blue, green, yellow, pink, or other cloaks; silk stockings; riding boots; pourpoints. Here, a king taking his oath; there, a king is abdicating; yet another shows a king signing a treaty; etc., etc., marrying, dying, etc. As for sculpture, it is unbelievable, one could easily count three thousand statues in the city. They are all the same. I proposed something quite simple to them. If the heads screwed on, they could be changed every two weeks, and they would only need about ten statues. A wit told them that foreigners only had one thing to fear in their town, and that it is to be made into statues.

When you come down to it, the Corneliuses, Kaulbachs, Schwinds, etc. have had their day, and Chenavard in particular. His painting inspired a good guffaw from everyone. As the Germans are very knowledgeable about that kind of painting, they found that all his figures and groupings are borrowed from Italian paintings. One of them was looking for figures stolen from the old masters in the painting. He said, 'You can recognize nearly all of them.' His neighbour answered, 'Unfortunately, treated like this, they are unrecognizable.'

Chenavard, Charles Blanc, and Couder created a big scandal in the Glyptothek, among the young people. The amazing trio was sitting on the steps of the monument in question bewailing the state of contemporary art. The three sages said, 'Kaulbach would put the entire exhibition in his mortar.'

The young people in Munich are doing well. I stayed a little longer for that reason. They have all decided to abandon all the old relics. I saw some young painters spit on the floor when they spoke of the princes of German art.

I have done five paintings in Munich, three copies – one of Frans Hals, a portrait by Velasquez, and Rembrandt's (Self portrait), all in their museum. I painted a female nude and a Tyrol landscape (Starnberg

Lake). I have painted six autumn landscapes with mountains since I have been in Switzerland. I leave tomorrow for Ornans.

G. Courbet

Rodin is defensive

Public commissions gave rise to countless disputes, to which Auguste Rodin was no stranger. The most notorious problems were with his fine memorial to Honoré de Balzac, now in the Boulevard Raspail, but which the sculptor never saw in place.

As for *The Burghers of Calais*, now happily installed on both sides of the English Channel in Calais and at Westminster, the preparatory study was subjected to various criticisms. This letter gives the sculptor's explicit views.[5]

My dear Chairman,

I have just been reading a note in the *Patriote de Calais* which repeats, more or less, the criticism already put forward, but which would emasculate my work; 'the heads should form a pyramid' (the method of Louis David) 'instead of a cube or a straight line'; this is simply the School laying down the law to me; *I am diametrically opposed to this principle*, which has prevailed in our period since the beginning of the century; it is diametrically opposed to the previous great periods of art, and the works conceived in this spirit are cold, lifeless, and conventional.

2. Eustache de Saint-Pierre seems to the critic to be in the presence of the king; so what are the men behind him supposed to be doing? No, he is leaving the town and going towards the camp; this is what gives the group the appearance of advancing, of movement. Eustache is the first to begin going down, and for my lines he has to be like that.

3. The monument is to be in a garden or in a monument designed by an architect. *It is to be in the middle of a square.*

The one who has lost heart and is plunged deep in thought alone may be altered; if you can keep it to that, my group is saved. These Gentlemen do not know that this is a model to a scale of one third, not a consultation with a view to beginning the work all over again.

In Paris I am the antagonist of this theatrical and School art. That would be wanting to make me the follower of people whose conventional art I despise.

Private patronage

Wilkie receives the Iron Duke

A private commission for a painting is statistically most likely to be for a portrait; but occasionally a picture of a particular subject is wanted, as this letter about the Duke of Wellington demonstrates.

In 1816 David Wilkie was at an early stage of his career. A visit from the hero of Waterloo was unexpected, but proved important, since a successful and popular picture resulted from it. Wilkie is writing to his friend Benjamin Haydon.

(to B. R. Haydon)[6] 18th August, 1816

. . . Yesterday Lord Lynedoch (Sir Thomas Graham that was) called upon me, and said that if I should be at home at four o'clock the Duke of Wellington and a party that came to meet at his house previous to that would then call on me with him. Upon this information I set to work for the rest of the day to get my rooms put to rights, put all my pictures in order for view, and last, though not least, had to arrange it so my mother and sister might see the great man from the parlour windows as he came in.

Matters being thus settled, we waited in a sort of breathless expectation for their arrival, and at half-past four they accordingly came. The party consisted of the Duke and Duchess of Bedford, Lady Argyle and another lady, the Duke of Wellington and Lord Lynedoch, to all of which the latter introduced me as they came in. When they went upstairs they were first occupied in looking at the pictures severally, but without entering into conversation further than by expressing a general approbation. The Duke, on whom my attention was fixed, seemed pleased with them, and said in his firm voice, 'Very good,' 'Capital,' &c. but said nothing in the way of remark, and seemed indeed not much attended to by the company, of whom the ladies began to talk a good deal. They went on in this way for a considerable time, and I had every reason to feel satisfied with the impression my works seemed to make on the Duke and Duchess of Bedford and the others, but though the Duke of Wellington seemed full of attention, I felt disappointed by his silence. At last Lady Argyle began to tell me that the Duke wished me to paint him a picture, and was explaining what the subject was, when the Duke, who was at that time seated on a chair and looking at one of the pictures that happened to be on the ground, turned to us, and swinging back upon the chair turned up his lively eye to me, and said that the subject should be a parcel of old soldiers assembled together on their seats at the door of a public-house, chewing tobacco and talking over their old stories. He thought they might be in any uniform, and that it should be at some public-house in the King's Road, Chelsea. I said this would make a most beautiful picture, and that it only wanted some story of principle incident to connect the figures together: he said perhaps playing at skittles would do, or any other game, when I proposed that one might be reading a newspaper aloud to the rest, and that in making a sketch of it many other incidents would occur. In this he perfectly agreed, and said I might send the sketch to him when he was abroad. He then got up and looked at his watch, and said to the company his time was nearly out, as he had to go and dine with the Duke of Cambridge.

After they had proposed to go, he made me a bow, and as he went out of the room he turned to me, and said, 'Well, when shall I hear from you?' To which I replied that my immediate engagements, and the time it would take to collect materials for his Grace's subject, would prevent me being able to get it done for two years. 'Very well,' said he, 'that will be soon enough for me.' They then went downstairs, and as they went out our people were all ready to see him from the parlour windows; when he got to the gate, he made me a bow again, and seeing at the same time my family at the parlour windows he bowed to them also. As he got upon his horse he observed all the families and the servants were at the windows, and I saw two lifeguards-men, the rogues, just behind the pillar at the corner, waiting for a full view of him.

The sensation this event occasioned quite unhinged us for the rest of the day. Nothing was talked of but the Duke of Wellington; and the chair he happened to sit upon has been carefully selected out, and has been decorated with ribbons, and there is talk of having an inscription upon it, descriptive of the honour it has received.

With respect to the appearance of the man, none of the portraits of him are like him. He is younger and fresher, more active and lively, and in his figure more clean-made and firmer built than I was led to expect. His face is in some respects odd; has not variety of expression, but his eye is extraordinary, and is almost the only feature I remember, but I remember it so well that I think I see it now. It has not the hungry and devouring look of Bonaparte, but seems to express in its liveliness the ecstasy that an animal would express in an active and eager pursuit.

Whistler and a patron

James Abbott McNeill Whistler was a heroic if quixotic personality in the art world, famous for his wit and his assertion of artists' independence. One of his celebrated disputes was with Sir William Eden about a portrait of Lady Eden, which he wrote about in *The Baronet and the Butterfly* which is mentioned here.

Whistler was a difficult man to deal with. Fortunately he felt a rapport with Charles Freer, the American industrialist and collector who was rich enough to indulge his liking for Whistler's work and formed an outstanding collection of it. The reference to Isaac Watts is for the poem, 'Against Quarrelling and Fighting', published in his *Divine Songs for Children*. The full verse is:

Let dogs delight to bark and bite,
For God has made them so,
Let bears and lions growl and fight,
For 'tis their nature to.

(to Charles Lang Freer)[7] — 29 July 1899, Pavillon Madeleine, Pourville-sur-mer, near Dieppe

I am delighted my dear Mr Freer that you like the pictures you speak of – and wish to keep them –

They are yours of course – and I will tell you when we meet how glad I am that they go to the group you have of distinguished work in your Gallery –

And now you must yield a point in proof of friendship and sympathy already proven!

Nothing is to be said about prices in this matter – until the Blue Girl takes her place to preside –

All this you will understand completely and feel with when we meet –

Meanwhile I think I may tell you without the least chance of being misunderstood, that I wish you to have a fine collection of Whistlers!! Perhaps *the* collection –

You see the Englishmen *have all* sold – 'for 'tis their nature to,' as Dr Watts beautifully puts it – whatever paintings of mine they possessed! directly they were hall-marked by the French Government, and established as of value, turning over, under my very eyes, literally for thousands what they had gotten for odd pounds! So that with the few exceptions that prove the rule, there is scarcely a canvas of mine left in the land! While you will understand the mischievous pleasure I have in 'constateing' this fact, & so placing the British Macaenas where he ought to be, behind the counter, and in his shop – you will also appreciate the lack of all communion between the artist and those who hold his work! and the great pleasure it gives him to look forward to other relations! –

I am glad you have the little *Cigale* – she is one of my latest pets – and of a rare type of beauty – the child herself I mean – and the painting – well the painting you see what I have said of it!!

The little Lady of Soho! I am glad you have chosen her too – I think before she is packed, I know of a touch I must add – and then she can follow you in the next steamer – But I shall see when I come over – for I am getting stronger and hope next week I may be able to cross – If the pictures have left the International, they will have gone to the 'Company of the Butterfly' 2. Hinde Street, Manchester Square.

So I enclose the order. I have written to Messrs Heinemann to send you my book! *The Baronet & the Butterfly* You must tell me how you like my campagne, if you think it worthy of West Point!
Always sincerely J. McNeill Whistler

Making a living

Public and private patronage apart, artists needed to find ways of making a living. For some, the answer was teaching, either as a full-time or part-time activity. For others, the century's newly efficient means of reproduction provided either income or employment. Fortunate artists had their work reproduced in steel engravings, adding considerably to the profit of painting a picture. The expansion of publishing gave employment to artists in book illustration, often linked as we have seen to work for magazines.

There were inevitably differences about how well engravers did their job of representing artists' intentions. Sometimes the discussions were amiable; Gérard, for example, wrote to his line engraver, Toschi, as follows: 'I have made numerous comments, but all on points of detail . . . I have to admit that most of these minor errors are my responsibility, and I ask it of your friendship as well as of your talent to put them right . . .'[8]

Constable had considerable difficulty with his set of mezzotints by David Lucas. Unfortunately they were not a financial success, which made the artist bitter when he reflected on the popularity of Turner's prints. Constable commented on a plate of 'Hadham Castle', 'I have not the wish to become the possessor of the large plate of the Castle, but I am anxious that it should be fine, & will take all pains with it. It will not fail of being so, if I may now judge.'[9]

But engravings not supervised by artists could be severely disappointing; Manet complained to François Flameng about a reproduction of one of his pictures in a catalogue and received an amazing reply:

'*Sir,* The engraving after *Le Bon Bock* is very bad because it is a good reproduction of the painting. I have, Sir, the honour to be, *Yours truly.*'[10]

William Blake also suffered disappointment when he tried to make a success of privately printed work; in 1818 he wrote to Dawson Taylor, including his price list for *Songs of Innocence* (three guineas for twenty-eight octavo prints) and *Songs of Experience* (twenty-six prints for the same price): 'The few I have printed and sold are sufficient to have gained me great reputation as an Artist, which was the chief thing Intended. But I have never been able to produce a Sufficient number for a general sale by means of a regular Publisher. It is therefore necessary to me that any Person wishing to have any or all of them should send me their Order to Print on the above terms, & I will take care that they shall be done at least as well as any I have yet produced.'[11]

Blake survived, though not in prosperity. There were others who gave up the struggle to be artists, but who were fortunate enough to have other talents. They could make distinctive if different careers, as William Hazlitt and Samuel Morse did.

Dahl refuses an appointment

Steady employment could be found in teaching; but there were difficulties for artists who wanted to develop their art in their own way. Johann Christian Dahl was born in Norway, but worked in Germany and Denmark. At the time of writing this extremely formal letter to the Director of Arts in Saxony, he was correct in asserting his position as a leading northern landscape painter, and in a good position to bargain for a Saxon pension, in addition to accepting a professorship in Copenhagen.

(to Count Vissthum von Eckstadt)[12] Dresden, 27 June 1828

A most humble memorandum

The more gracious and honourable are the sentiments with which Your Excellency has designed to accept my humble request of March 21st, the more painful it is for me to have to decline your gracious offer of the academic chair of landscape painting to be established here at the Academy.

Your Excellency being a great patron of the arts and familiar with the peculiarities of the artistic temperament, it emboldens me to speak my mind freely to you regarding my views. I do so only now, because it is only now that I have been able to make a full assessment and exposition of my reasons; I felt obliged to await more detailed information for which I had asked in previous letters concerning the circumstances in Copenhagen, which had not been made clear to me and which I have only now received.

May your Excellency condescend to vouchsafe with your customary indulgence these my ideas, which are of course open to correction.

The artist in my opinion must in his artistic life follow his own genius implicitly. He cannot accept anything foreign to his nature without disadvantage to his art, and he therefore should not take on any responsibilities which might inhibit the free flow of his individuality.

I am quite certain that as far as my own peculiar qualities are concerned, with the best will in the world, it would have a distracting and depressing effect on me if I had to tie my academic teaching to the clock, if I may so express it; often in the midst of my enthusiasm for some subject, I should have to remind myself not to miss my class. At the same time I should be teaching more in painting studios than in nature, with some talented students perhaps, but possibly more students without a vocation to train in art.

Were I, as might be, the only professor of landscape, I should be afraid that, as a painter more of northern land and seascapes, I should give a wrong direction to all those whose talent is more of the southern skies; this despite paying the most scrupulous regard to their individual requirements, simply because of my independence and solitary habit of work. In my present teaching conditions, anyone who does not feel attracted to my idiosyncracies is at liberty to follow the guidance of a different landscape painter. Often I have myself recommended this course to my students after a period of teaching, so that they learn to follow their own genius, rather than that of another, and continue to develop their own originality. In so doing they become, not disciples of a school, but disciples of nature, which recognises neither school nor style.

All my apprehensions voiced hitherto fall away in the case of the post offered in Copenhagen. I know this to be so not only as a result of the afore-mentioned letters and the letter just received, but also from several previous visits to Copenhagen. In any case the professors there need devote only a few evening lessons every three months to formal academic teaching. They need attend only now and then, and the nude is posed only three times a month. There, without having to leave the building, I should be able to go from my work and studio to the lecture theatre and still be able to carry on working in the same state of mind. On occasion I might have to beg a colleague to take my class.

Incidentally, all members of the Academy have equal rights, which is not permitted in our constitution here. Everyone has a voice in conferences, and all members form a single body. No one is subordinate to anyone else and no individual may object if the pupils of another teacher want to attend drawing or life-classes for a longer period as soon as a place becomes vacant. Thus everyone has the opportunity to observe his students also, which would not be permitted in our Academy here, not even to a professor of landscape painting. All these reasons taken together confirm me in my clear conviction that I must not accept an established academic chair at the Academy here.

Much as I feel in duty bound to give the most respectful thanks to His Royal Majesty and Your Excellency for the very highest grace and favour which I have been able to enjoy for so long, and much as I would wish to be of further use in diverse ways to this, my beloved second fatherland, yet I believe I owe it to the peculiarities of my genius as a more nordic and nautical painter to perfect myself and to take up the invitation from Copenhagen, if His Majesty for the aforementioned purpose would graciously deign to grant me a supplement of 300 Thaler so that there may be no alteration in my present style of living as befits a teacher.

Once again I beg Your Excellency most respectfully to receive my present humble suggestion with your customary grace and, if possible, to support my respectful petition to His Majesty.

In deep reverence I remain Your Excellency's obedient servant.

J. C. Dahl

Hazlitt and the bootmaker

Some who tried to become artists did not succeed, and among them was William Hazlitt. He started out as a portrait painter, but the picture mentioned in the following letter was said to have been 'sent home with an abusive letter' from the young man's mother. Hazlitt fortunately was able to pay his bills with his earnings as a writer, which included some art criticism and his entertaining *Conversations with James Northcote RA* (1830).

(to Thomas Hardy, bootmaker)[13] May or June 1811

Sunday evening. Winterslow, Salisbury

I was obliged to leave London without discharging my promise, the reason of which was that I was myself disappointed in not receiving £20 which was due to me, £10 for a picture, and £10 for revising a manuscript. I am at present actually without money in the house. If you can defer til October, when I shall be in London to deliver some Lectures, by which I shall pick up some money, I shall esteem it a favour, and shall be glad to pay you the interest from the time I was in London last. Hoping this delay will be no particular inconvenience, and that you will think it unavoidable on my part, I remain, yours respectfully,

W. Hazlitt

Morse has a dream

Another failed painter was an eminently successful man of business and invention. Samuel Morse is still remembered for the signalling code which he invented.

In this letter he is replying many years after he had given up the practice of art to a letter from James Fenimore Cooper whose best known book, *The Last of the Mohicans* was published in 1826.

(to James Fenimore Cooper)[14] November 20, 1849

Alas! My dear sir, the very name of *pictures* produces a sadness of heart I cannot describe. Painting has been a smiling mistress to many, but she has been a cruel jilt to me. I did not abandon her, she abandoned me. I have scarcely taken any interest in painting for many years. Will you believe it? When last in Paris, in 1845, I did not go into the Louvre, nor did I visit a single picture gallery.

I sometimes indulge a vague dream that I may paint again. It is rather the memory of past pleasures, when hope was enticing me onward only to deceive me at last. Except some family portraits, valuable to me from their likenesses only, I could wish that every picture I ever painted was destroyed. I have no wish to be remembered as a painter. My ideal of that profession was, perhaps, too exalted – I may say is too exalted. I leave it to others more worthy to fill the niches of art.

Caldecott and an author

A sedate type of commissioned work was book illustration, which in the hands of a gifted draughtsman could be successful both artistically and financially. Randolph Caldecott had the qualities needed for success in the field of children's books.

One of his collaborators was Juliana Horatio Ewing, with whom he did three books. The following letter is about *Daddy Darwin's Dovecot.* Caldecott also mentions his *Picturebooks*, of which he drew sixteen and for which he is best known.

(to Juliana Horatio Ewing)[15] Broomfield, Frensham, Farnham, Surrey
6 July 1884

My dear Mrs Ewing,
Here are 2 drawings corrected. I have taken out and put in again the face of the young lady and boys and have added terrier. I have also taken out and reput in chin and eye of young lady in garden. (I have also made the chin lighter in Phoebe Shaw returning from the church; but I do not return it for inspection). And *all* this in warm weather and with hay still about. Better if you had had the drawings in the month of April! You are not even decided yet – process or engraving? I wished to know which before making the drawings – I should not have used white for process.

Your letter is interesting because of the remark about my heroines having passed their first youth and I feel quite pleased that you have made it. Mrs R. C. is – and has been – of this opinion – and so I am to a great extent. But the instance which you give – p. 17, 'Milkmaid' – I do not feel to be applicable. I have smoked a cigarette over it and I consider the girl to be only about 20 – and the mother in the frontispiece to be old enough to have a son of 17.

And I cannot allow that the parson's daughter was not – before alteration to face and figure – quite correct for 19. I am not saying she was nice; but, according to my experience, possible and even common. The healthy country people that I have known – milkmaids and parsons' daughters – have been quite women at 19. And I maintain that although I seldom represent, or try to represent, girls of 15 or 16, yet my young women are seldom more than 25 – generally about 20 – and at 20 the first bloom of youth is certainly over. You will smile at my assured way of putting it. I find that many artists – illustrators – fight shy of representing the age of 15 or 16. It is, however, a difficult thing to draw small faces in ink so that all observers shall agree as to the age represented. And 'figures' vary so much that one cannot lay down laws about them.

I may remark here that milkmaids in the dairy districts that I know do not marry as early as those in your experience. What you say of chins is true – I make a note of it – but the suggestion to 'give a touch more size to the eyes' makes one think that one must be careful in accepting – or rather in acting upon – criticisms of this kind. Mr Blackburn used to say that I was the only man who would alter – I like to do so when I am sure it would be better, although the certainty may be forced upon me by a critic who regards things with different eyes from mine. I have altered the eye of the lady in question: but I have made it rather smaller. It was monstrously large before and not in its right place. It is a very cheap way of making a pretty face to draw large eyes, and then the effect is not intellectual, unless the brow is massive – which will tend to give an imp-like look to the head. Of imps there are 2 kinds – small-brained and large-brained.

I have always been struck by the truthful value given to faces by artists who know how to keep down the eyes. Du Maurier is good in this way – Leech was not so in female faces – in *woodcuts* – and they often looked rather silly.

If I had enlarged the eye in question the distance from the eyebrow to under-lid would have been greater than distance from under-lid to bottom of nostril.

Pardon me for going into these details: as you are a good and valued friend I can pardon myself.

P.S. Monday morning 8.30

I wrote somewhat hastily and jerkily yesterday and now I see that I have forgotten several things. The post-boy has not yet come – so I will scribble further.

Do not think I have been doing your work hurriedly or carelessly. The drawing of *D. D. and P. daughter* is one of 5 made, and I was obliged to let one go at last.

The proofs about Tiny and Toby I return. I am much obliged to you for offering its illustration to me, but I really cannot go into the question beyond saying that I cannot undertake anything more – however small – at present.

I have time to add that of all dogs – all kinds of dogs – I think I have least sympathy with pugs. I have very little sympathy with the kind of human people they seem to me to represent in the doggy world.

You will do me a service if you will always be kind enough to say what you think about drawings – in detail and generally. Some people let one drift to ruin by not giving true opinions.

R. C.

7

THE TRAVELLERS

The nineteenth century saw a tremendous range of new opportunities for travel – to the carriages and coaches of the previous age were added the railway, the bicycle, and tentative uses for the internal combustion engine, while at sea sail-power gave way to steam. Not that artists always needed or wanted to use the new means of travel. A sketching artist might prefer to walk to choose his subjects; and poverty induced students to walk, as the Flandrin brothers walked to Paris from Lyon to join Ingres' studio. Travelling into little known territory was likely to be on horseback, as letters from Delacroix and Remington will remind us. Nevertheless, this was a century in which the pace of life quickened, and where the artist played a role in spreading knowledge about what the world and its peoples looked like. We also have valuable evidence from letters about what artists felt.

Professional travel

Some artists travelled for clearly defined professional reasons, looking at art, meeting other artists, or assessing opportunities for work. Knowledge of foreign languages was an asset, and our first letter is from a young Parisian who was taught English by a friend.

Delacroix tries out his English

Delacroix was eighteen when he first made friends with Charles Raymond Soulier, who had been brought up in London, but returned to Paris where his occupations included giving English lessons. Incidentally, Soulier was able to tell Delacroix about watercolour technique, at that time little understood in France.

(to Charles Raymond Soulier)[1] Forêt de Boixe, septembre 1820.

Dear friend,

You must not wonder at my slowness in writing you. From Paris, I gone first to Tours to meet a little with my brother I have not seen long since. I lived here about fifteen days, and not was possible to write any thing in English for I wanted English books or dictionaries. Moreover and to tell the truth, I should be equally diverted from my purpose by the continual feasts and entertainments. I left him at last. But during my journey to my dear forest, I was seized by a devilish fever, which takes away all my pleasure in country. I live tristly long days, without any stomach. I see with impatiernce from my window the murmuring trees and singing birds. But nor the barking dogs in sonorous groves, nor the raising sun with all its splendor refresh my senses or rejoice them. I am a slave confined in a house; when I attempt to read or write any thing, my head is so full of tediousness, so feeble and heavy upon my shoulders, that I am very soon forced to forsake all business. You shall discern without difficulty how much is hard and pitful my english linguage. Nevertheless I find a mere pleasure in writing you. I hope you shall excuse the mistakes and errors; I am so idle and disconforted, when I must search a word in the dictionary that there is no doubt I put imprudently a great deal of improper words. – Through my lucid moments, I take my faithful Richard III who was not, I believe, so sweet and delightful to his brothers, nephews and attendants, that to my mind and in my hands. I know not for what reason this tragedy is not placed in number of the betters of Shakespeare. I own there are some long things and needless, but there is always to be felt the talent of the author in the living painting and investigation of secret motions of human heart.

Eastlake in Italy

Italy, as we have seen, had a special attraction for British artists, no less than for Germans and the French; one visitor to Italy was Charles Eastlake whose vivacious response to his new experiences are here described to his friend Benjamin Haydon. In this letter Eastlake's review of the different national schools of art is in its way as remarkable as the unbuttoned comments on Florentine sculpture.

(to Benjamin Haydon)[2]

If I had written to you from Florence, which I thought of doing, I might have been able to describe my feelings on seeing that city and its contents. You cannot have an idea of Michel Angelo without going there. He is the genius of the place and meets you everywhere. Not Rome itself can give you more delight than the thousand objects of interest that you meet there. In every street are either busts or statues of the Medici, or the 'palle': their arms ornament the walls. I even observed these arms on the back of an old chair at an inn before I arrived in Florence. You turn into the great square; at a distance some white figures against the old palace look like colossal paintings, you soon find them to be marble statues and recognise Michel Angelo's 'David', with an arm and a wrist such as he alone could have sculptured, and looking twice as strong as a great 'Hercules', by Bandinelli, close by.

There are the masterworks of all the sculptors there, and all more or less fine, except an unhappy giant in a fountain, said to be by Ammanati. In the chapel of the Medici all of Michel Angelo's best, but the number of unfinished things by him is quite curious. You see him in some of these things, after having blocked out an arm in the roughest way, indulging himself with finishing a bit of the hand and just hatching round the thumb, and some parts quite soft and two or three sharp touches, leaving it – for ever. One thinks him less a Mannerist after seeing these things. No marble was ever so like flesh, except the Elgin figures. Momentary actions are attempted, and most successfully, and the uniform tension objected to in him does not strike one here, or looks like a latent strength. The thigh of the 'Night', in G. de' Medici's tomb, is the most wonderful thing of this sort. Though she be asleep you fancy she will dart her leg out with force enough to knock a house down, so 'heaped with strength and turned with elegance'. You think of nothing but muscle before any figure of Michel

Angelo's. You see masses of it slipping about. I was going to say you hear the tendons crack – but, after all, he seems rather to give the idea of the power of motion than of motion itself, and the motion of knocking down than of leaping, etc. The colossal size helps all this and the proportions of his extremities, which are in a sort of sledge-hammer taste, so that, putting his invention out of the question, there is a certain degree of terror inspired even by his forms. I could have explained my notions better at the time. I suppose you will hardly understand this. You ought not to rest until you have seen Michel Angelo and Florence. I just now think you have not latterly trod so closely in his steps, as I think your natural taste would lead you to Rubens. Rembrandt and the Elgin Marbles have all conspired in different ways to change your judgment on this subject.

I have a notion that the Bolognese colour and a certain degree of Michel Angelo's bursting strength, added to the nimble elegance of the Greek statues, would produce a style more congenial to your feelings. The English taste, too, may have some influence. The English is now the first school of colour in the world. This is all right enough, but it is quite certain the sort of nature as man must study for colour must narrow his feelings in form. And the Hoppners and Romneys, who would say Michel Angelo is 'unnatural,' are not to be taken as oracles from the practice they have both omitted and committed; or, to be more polite, the very nature of their merit implies, as men study in England, a more than ordinary neglect and ignorance of the higher parts of their Art.

The French are put out of the question on all hands as destitute of feeling for painting; the Italians are weak; the Germans and the English are the only two sensible schools, and yet nothing can be more opposite! There are hosts of Germans here determined to restore the mind of the Art; they paint in fresco; they study Masaccio; and in their bad works are like Albert Dürer. They have no idea of colour or effect, but, for dignity and truth of expression, and the motive of their figures, I think their Art ranks very high. They must get out of their absurdities in time. These are so striking, especially to an English eye, that when I first saw some of their works I thought them without merit.

I now think they have the highest, but still not what one would follow. They should be judged of from their drawings, some of which I think are equal to anything that has been done in invention, expression and general propriety. The English are devoted to mere imitation of substances, save and except that imperceptible thing which arises out of practice. They are aware of no principle in Art; to copy what you see is perfection, and they make a head round and coming from the picture. The Germans say the same, always supposing selection, and they imitate an expressive turn of the head and the looks and actions of nature. Their colour and effect are below criticism. Some of these Germans have restored not only the Art, but the dress of the fifteenth century. You meet Raphael's costume in the streets. The number of these painters is such that all foreigners, until lately, were called Tedeschi! The host of English that have poured into Rome, and the magnificence they display, have given the natives a high idea of us, especially after the bombardment of Algiers, which is now exhibiting at a theatre here, where, I am told, the nine Muses dance about Lord Exmouth! The Dey of Algiers sings a bravura, &c.

I saw Canova by accident in the street before I went to deliver your letter, and as I introduced myself to him by saying that I had brought a letter from you, I thought it needless to use the letter afterwards. He lives like a king, and is difficult of access. The democracy he talked to you of is an aristocracy of artists.

Yours ever, C. L. Eastlake.

Bonheur buys models

Rosa Bonheur was in mid-career in 1856, when she was persuaded by her dealer Ernest Gambart to visit Scotland. Gambart rightly judged that the existing British market for his artist's work could be further developed.

Rosa Bonheur was delighted with her picturesque trip, and as the letter to her household explains, she enjoyed a successful buying spree.

(to Mme Peyrol)[3] August 1856

Here I am back from my gad about the Highlands. For just a month we have been climbing mountains and crossing waters without resting. I am about tired. Ah! why can't I show you, my dear Juju, all the fine things I have seen? I must, at any rate, tell you about them by word of mouth. I have seen all the places Walter Scott has chosen for the characters he has created, especially those of the 'Legend of Montrose', which I have just been reading. I have been to Argyll Castle where Mary Stuart was born, and I visited it from top to bottom; Edinburgh also, a most picturesque town where it rains too often. At present I know Scotland pretty well. You meet with nothing but MacGeorges, Macdonalds, and Macs of all sorts, real bare-legged mountaineers, and big Englishmen, who travel in opera costumes in order to pose as heroes. In fine, I will relate you my excursions and tell you my stories by Mammy's fireside, while smoking cigarettes, which I am longing to do.

I arrived yesterday at Mr Gambart's country house, after a twenty-hours' sea voyage. You see that I am quite experienced, and shall be able one of these days to go sketching to America or China. I am bringing back a cargo, not of studies, but of living animals, of which I intend to make some fine pictures, if I can. I have a bull, two cows, two young bulls, four sheep, and a calf. They are so picturesque and their colour so beautiful that I should like to paint them all at the same time. I mean to peg away as if my life depended on it. In fact, I have all I want, except sufficient time. In a word, I am in ecstasies over what I have seen. But a rolling stone gathers no moss, and I haven't collected much in the way of studies. I must make it up with the animals, which have cost me dear, although I bought them cheaper than in France. I shouldn't like to fail with a single one, they are so beautiful to paint.

Kiss your little brat for me. I wanted to buy him a little Highland costume, it suits children so well. But this shall be for next time.

Manet visits Madrid

Another traveller abroad for professional reasons was Edouard Manet. In 1865 his *Olympia* was accepted at the Paris Salon, but provoked sharp hostile criticism. Manet decided to visit Spain, where he expected to find that the example of Velasquez would reinforce his search for a personal style of direct painting unlike the high finish of academic art.

His letter is to Henri Fantin-Latour, a firm ally who had been a fellow exhibitor two years before. This was at a show of pictures which had been turned down by the Salon jury; the Emperor Napoleon III had ordered that all the refused works should be shown together in an exhibition of rejects, a *Salon des Refusés*.

(to Henri Fantin-Latour)[4] Madrid [August ?] 1865

My dear fellow,
How I miss you here, and how delighted you would have been to see Velasquez, who in himself is worth the journey. The painters of all other schools, who surround him in the Madrid Gallery, and are very well represented there, all seem like *chiqueurs*. He is the painter of painters. He did not astonish me, but delighted me. The full-length portrait we have in the Louvre is not by him. Only the Infanta is beyond question. Here there is an enormous picture, full of little figures like those in the picture in the Louvre called 'Les Cavaliers'; but figures of men and women, perhaps better, and above all, quite untouched by the restorer. The background, a landscape, is by a pupil of Velasquez.

The most astonishing item among his splendid work, and perhaps the most astonishing ever painted, is the picture listed in the catalogue as 'Portrait of a famous Actor in the reign of Philip IV'. The background disappears; it is simply air that surrounds the man, dressed all in black and alive. And the 'Spinners', the fine portrait of Alonzo Cano, 'Las Meninas', another extraordinary picture! The philosophers, astonishing things! All the dwarfs; one in particular, seated, full face, his fists on his hips; just the painting for a real connoisseur. His magnificent portraits; one would like to mention everything; there are none but masterpieces. A portrait of Charles V, by Titian, which has a great reputation that must be deserved, and which I should certainly have thought good anywhere else, looks wooden here.

And Goya! The most curious after the master he imitated too closely, imitated in the most servile sense of the word. Great zest, though. There are two fine equestrian portraits by him in the gallery, in the style of Velasquez, but much inferior. What I have seen of his so far has not pleased me overmuch. In the next few days I am to see a magnificent collection of his work belonging to the Duke of Ossuna.

I am disconsolate; the weather looks very ugly this morning and I fear this evening's bull-fight, to which I have been looking forward, may be postponed. Until when? Tomorrow I go to Toledo. There I shall see Greco and Goya, who I am told are very well represented.

Madrid is a pleasant town, full of entertaining things. The Prado is a charming public walk, crowded with pretty women, all in mantillas, which gives it a very original appearance. In the streets one still sees many national costumes; the toreros, too, have a curious street dress.

Farewell, my dear Fantin, I shake your hand and am yours very truly.

E. Manet

A realist assesses the competition

Ilya Repin was sent to study abroad by the Russian Academy of Fine Arts, and when writing this letter had reached Italy. Here he is replying to a painter and critic whom he admired and who was a leading supporter of realism in Russian art.

(to I. N. Kramskoy)[5] August 21, 1873
Albano

I have received your letter, dear Ivan Nikolaevitch, when I was going to leave for Albano (where I am at the moment). This is actually the reason of my being slow with the answer. It is quite a mass, because I have written you many imaginable letters with numerous descriptions of impressions, which are generously given to anybody by a trip.

We are at the place for five days already. We are enjoying new places for a stroll (they are wonderful, like ours, but more picturesque). We had a lot of new problems to solve and I have just found time to answer you.

First, thank you very much. I didn't expect so much attention to me (two large pages). You won't probably understand this and might even suspect me of being ironical. One has to live for almost three months in Italy, meeting no people of the same interests and the same (so to say) life, to value your cordiality, your open smile, your written embrace. I am shaking your hand with all my heart.

Second, I shall try to answer all your questions.

I shall give you only a brief statement on Vienna. It is Europe, but if one looks more attentively it is only Europe's inn. Everything is made for a brief tour, for a quick look of the foreigner. Even fine art museums (Belveder) are full of bad copies, which are nevertheless shamelessly said to be originals ('They will never notice, they are in a hurry').

A few words about the Vienna exhibition (I hope it won't look like looking for raspberries in autumn, and that you haven't heard more than I am going to tell). I had a strong impression, a stunning one from Matejko's pictures, especially from two of them and the third one at the Belveder. What drama! What force! His paintings are hanging very high, but they overpower everything, so that nothing looks interesting after them. (I shan't describe the pictures, it will be dull to read.) Only Regnault, the Frenchman can be compared with him (the mounted figure), but nobody is superior in painting.

I can remember now many pictures but I can't remember their authors (I was there for a short time and didn't feel well, I could hardly look at the pictures). There is a lot of freshness and ingeniousness, a lot of courage, a lot of enthusiasm and energy. They grasp imagination, grasp nature as it exists. They reject the yoke of routine, but don't think that it has disappeared. No, it still reigns in the hall *d'honneur* and proudly smooths creased clothes like Italian clergy. Oh, how lazy I am, how superficial, not a single fact mentioned! The only consolation is in our having, of course, plenty of it. 'Assassination of Julius Caesar' (looks almost like a copy from Camuccini), plafonds by Cabanel. My God! Is there any justice somewhere, at least in art? What are all these things doing in the halls of fame? Nevertheless, everything is right, and even Piloty's huge picture deserves it.

It's surprising, how he, after such inner truth of life as 'Death of Wallenstein' appears to be, could fall to such routine, to weakness of copying Makart. But there are beautiful things on the different heights and in the different corners, the pictures of life as it is, without addition of deep knowledge of art, of author.

Let's take this one as an example. It's dawn, the narrow street of a gothic town is buried in snow, in the wet snow. Snow has indifferently covered the pavement, the entrance of the monastery and the corpse of the Count murdered at the monastery gate at night. The monks got up early in the morning, opened the gate and gasped observing a dead body at the gate. Everything is real as in life, and sometimes I have a feeling that I have seen it not in the frame under the ceiling of the huge hall but on my way in a German town. I still can see the street and a dead body covered with wet snow. Everybody was interested with pictures by Defregger and Knaus.

Of course, they work hard, forgetting about themselves, ecstatically. Unfortunately they often forget to think, in which case they are rescued only by abundance of practice, by their love for images and by their courage. Of course, there are plenty of good plots, compositions, but it doesn't touch.

Finally, in spite of many outstanding things, of many strong instruments, which were mastered, I come to the conclusion that fine art is lagging behind the other arts, which not only keep pace with the intellectually growing people, but even act as a guideline for these people (literature). I forgot to tell you about sculpture. Monteverde (the Italian, I have visited him in his studio in Rome) is wonderful, his 'Vaccinator', 'Young Columbus', 'Franklin's genius' (fantasie) and 'Children with a cat' are marvellous things!

Nevertheless, something is wrong with it. The art seems to have renounced life, to have no notion of the environment. It swells, tortures itself, makes up funny plots, tales, fables, dives into the old times, tried even attempting subjects and thinks 'Now I've guessed'. No, even now the public only feels surprised and uncomfortable.

Next, Repin replies to a passage in Kramskoy's letter about a German's opinion of 'Towing by the Volga';

'He was very witty at defining the idea of your picture: "a small group of people belonging to the dying out tribe, which is rather savage and close to gorilla, being approached by the civilization (steamer)." Isn't that lovely! And quite true by the way! What would you say about this?'

And the German. What a judgement! Precise. Germans will be Germans. The ideas of humanity seem to him a trifle, he longs for absolute idea, he is interested only in organic and geological matters – pure philosopher. We haven't yet had a chance to get acquainted with Germans. The Austrians haven't gone far from Italians. We haven't seen a single intellectual face in Vienna, the best representatives resemble tobacconists (in Italy they look like barbers). I should say, nevertheless, that all my conclusions are fairly superficial. . . .

What can I tell you about Polenov? He is a very pleasant chap, and I liked him even more in Italy. It was especially pleasant for me to find a friend in abusing Italy and Italy lovers. We were unburdening our hearts during those conversations. When I arrived, he had already packed. I haven't seen his works here. Only at Naples he showed me some with a great deal of jokes and laughter. He is a good friend. We dream about our future perspectives at home. However, Praskhov and

Antokolsky's opinion about him isn't very high, they call him a 'log'. All the same I think he is talented and has good taste. He only lacks independence a little . . .

Impressions

An artist's impressions of a foreign country could be vivid and entertaining to a correspondent, whether describing incidents and places or just the mood of a journey. Extracts of this sort could be indefinitely multiplied; just a handful have been selected, incidentally documenting two new means of travel, the transatlantic liner and the bicycle.

Gavarni dreams in London

During the 1840s and 1850s the flow of European illustrated papers was in spate. The period saw the rise of satirical or humorous papers such as *Punch* and *Simplicissimus*; it was also a start for visual reportage on, say, the *Illustrated London News*, for which Gavarni worked. This letter with a light touch is written to a friend in Paris.

(to Louis Leroy)[6] London 1848

What am I doing in London? I am dreaming, working and dreaming. Every morning I have a shot at reforming the cosmos (I no longer concern myself with the world of politics – I settled that long ago). I ask myself, for example, whether, when one comes to think of it, it would really be worthwhile for the inhabitants of our planet to visit the Moon, whether the journey would be worth the trouble of seeing how it can be arranged. – Pooh! it's only a trifle – but I have so little spare time . . .

You want some 'travel impressions'; tonight, at this Drury Lane ball, something utterly fantastic happened to me. – In the first place, you must imagine one of those fine balls such as we have at the Opera, without the hoi polloi, – a fancy dress ball, as sumptuous as, for example, some evening-dress balls before or just after 1830. – Lights, satin, diamonds and a tremendous crush – (it was not a public ball); – the orchestra occupied the back half of the stage, and behind the orchestra a suite of rooms had been kept free – rooms with gold-embroidered muslin hangings, huge mirrors and soft divans on which women sat here and there. – I strolled through, looking at everything; – coming to one of the last rooms, I walked across to a big curtained door leading to another apartment full of more sofas and more people. I was horribly fatigued, even unwell, and dragged myself over to this last corner so as to have seen everything before going home to bed. By chance the door was unencumbered, an open space between two crowds. – So on I went, peering through my lorgnette, and as I cross the threshold I found myself face to face, nose to nose, with a person who was also peering through his lorgnette – and could not understand, at first, why, since the door was a wide one, this unknown fellow (in morning dress) was walking straight into me. – We looked at each other, – his was a disagreeable expression; the man's face was pale and sweating, he had a beard I thought tousled and too long, – and there was something horrible, yet sad in the whole cast of his countenance. – I remembered! this was the dreadful face that was printed in one of the numbers of the [*Illustrated*] *London News* last January; – and then at last, waking up completely, I realized it was *I*. – Drowsiness was leading me into a mirror, my back turned to the group of women I had been going to see. Those white ladies must have thought: 'What a conceited Frenchman!'

There, my good Louis, you see what work, the incessant vibration of thought, that magic cord which runs on two pulleys, the head and the heart, and wears them out – you see what gin, stout and disturbing celibacy have reduced your friend to. – A thousand affectionate compliments to your gracious mistress.

An American on Merseyside

Edwin Austin Abbey reached the Mersey on board the *Germanic* on December 17, 1878. These were his first impressions of England, where he was to make his reputation as an illustrator and a historical painter, and, as we have seen, was to be elected a Royal Academician. This is a family letter.[7]

I look around for the first time upon someone else's country. I see a high bank covered with light snow, rows of houses sort of terraced up, a battery of stone with short towers at the corners. Everything looks dirty; water is dirty, boats that we pass are beastly dirty, sails almost black. I'm looking away and talking to the Professor about these things, when – down comes the fog, and in less time than it takes to say so, denser than ever, and the tooting and ringing begins again. Chilly, damp and disagreeable again. We back and wait for about fifteen minutes. Then the fog lifts a little and right back of us is the landing stage – a long flat with house on it and bridges going up on the quay. We tumble off again, and are immediately accosted by the dirtiest newsboys I ever saw, and bootblacks – and for the first time I saw a 'Bobby'. Oh! Such a funny one. Really his face was so ridiculously like a caricature mask that I thought at first he had one on. All the people look so different somehow – they shuffle about; the boys all wear caps – all ragged and all with small scarfs lightly tied around their necks, and the police keeping them out of the way. Newsboys with big printed placards of news hanging in front of them. Ticket posters, real 'Toby Vecks' with brass labels tied on their arms, all in sleeved waistcoats, all with big, heavy, ugly feet and red noses – all small, and all old. Old men with funny-shaped plug hats and black ribbon about their necks, all the poor people with mud up to their armpits. And certainly the poorest people I ever saw. I would never have believed that people would go about looking so desperately wretched. Our tramps are princes to them. They seem to be lame, most of them – anyway they nearly all jam their hands away down in their pockets, and limp. I think of 'Poor Jo', I think of Fildes' 'Casual Ward' at the Centennial, of Leech's pictures in Dickens – of Charles Keene.

The appeal of old England to Abbey is well expressed in a letter written eleven years later. He was staying with John Singer Sargent and his family and other friends at Fladbury Rectory.

19 September, 1889[7]

Early on Tuesday I drove over to Fladbury, taking my belongings, and in the afternoon I began the background of my picture the 'Callers', and have progressed well with it. . . .

It is only two people come to make a call and sitting in front of the old red-brick house, with roses growing over it, and a maid in pink calico taking in their cards. It has no intellectual quality whatever in its conception. . . . I got tired of everything I was doing, and this rests

me. I have worked hard both the afternoons and in the mornings. I have been making sketches in Cropthorne Church. One I shall use for *The Deserted Village*. It is a beautiful old place, with grey carved pews – old pews, Gothic ones – and there are good monuments. I shall do, I think, a little watercolour of a girl sitting in church. . . . The colour is charming. . . . an old pale stone tomb, with two (full-length recumbent figures) heads on pillows and several of the sons (they seem to have had eighteen children) straggling around the corner, for whom there is no room in front. The wall behind her (the girl) is whitewashed, and the pew is of grey wood – green out of the window. Cropthorne is full of beautiful bits, and it is nice to go to, to see . . .
(Added in London) I am sitting in the beautiful big library of the Reform, and it is growing late in the dull autumn day. It is drizzling outside, and the big chestnut trees out of the window in Carlton Gardens are dripping. The room is big and shadowy, the gilded bindings on the bookshelves gleam faintly in the dusk, and the gilded flutings of the green columns shine dimly all down the long, dim places. A few old gentlemen are dozing over their books, and one or two others are writing away like mad; and the rumbling of wheels away off somewhere are the only sounds . . .

Adams-Acton and the Pope

Colonel The O'Gorman Mahon, a remarkable Irishman, persuaded the sculptor John Adams-Acton to visit Rome with him on the understanding that a commission for a bust of Pope Leo XIII could be arranged. So it was.

Here is an incident recorded by the sculptor about the two friends on their way to the Papal audience. Incidentally, the trick with a pair of gloves has a more modern parallel in Picasso's early life.

(to his wife)[8] Rome, December 7th (1882)

I forgot to tell you in my last letter that we went to the Vatican to pay our homage to the Holy Father in one pair of white kid gloves between us! I always have a pair of white kid gloves in my dress-coat pocket, but on my way to the Vatican I found by some means they had disappeared, and it was rather a disappointment to see the Colonel toyed out in a grand new pair. I made a remark about it, and the

Colonel said 'You can have *one* of mine if you like.' – 'Right!' said I, so one was handed to me, and we went in, to all appearances perfectly equipped, until we came to the room next to the Audience Chamber, then, to our astonishment, one of the Masters of Ceremony came up to us and pointing to our one glove on each hand (sic) said 'Gloves are not allowed to be worn in the presence of the Holy Father!' so after all our contrivance they were no use to us!

I hope soon to get a command to take my bust, which I am now working on, up to the Vatican for a sitting.

Today we went outside the Porta Pia to see the church of St Agnese and the Christian Catacombs. It is a beautiful early Christian church built over an old temple of Bacchus. The catacombs are the oldest in Rome and the most extensive. Several skeletons now mouldering to dust we saw, and I was astonished to see the teeth in such perfect preservation – most beautiful and perfect in their shape and as white and polished as living teeth.

Sturge Moore goes cycling

Sight-seeing in the 1890s could take the form of a cycling tour, an attractive way of compounding joy with economy. In August 1897 a plan to visit French cathedrals was suggested by the sculptor Henry Poole to Thomas Sturge Moore 'to cost not more than £5 a head and to last not more than a week.'

Sturge Moore as a wood engraver had been working closely with Charles Ricketts and Charles Shannon, whose Vale Press was started in 1896. He was also a dramatist and poet, the main sphere of his work throughout his life. Sturge Moore's account of his trip with Henry Poole follows; they began by travelling overnight to Dieppe and headed for Amiens. He is writing to an early friend.

(to A. H. Fisher)[9]

We passed through the forest of Eu in fine weather with Puvis de Chavannes opening out on either hand . . . on we went and soon came to the most wonderful place we were to see – Rambures, an old village stretching some half mile along a cross road with houses on one side of the valley only; immense woods immediately behind it and in front; the church alone faced the other buildings and stood in a wilderness of half gilded, half rusted iron crosses, to which hung white glass wreaths etc. Everything was just as one would desire it and a few yards further on the trees opened up on one side and through some park gates we caught a glimpse of a chateau. Four solid Norman towers of red brick planted so close together there hardly seems room for anything between them. However, out of this massive calix there rose a little Mont St Michel of pointed roofs and turret chimneys, the four pepper-box Norman towers being quite dominated by its flowerlike elegance. The whole stood back like an elephant in the water with a Queen's houdah on its back . . .

In Amiens our host was a big man with red hair and the longest moustaches I have ever seen, these when he ate or worked he wound round his ears. We climbed all over the Cathedral, where the concierge remembered Ruskin who always complained of being ill yet was always working hard. . . . The rose windows are like sea weeds spread out under a rich still sea to a perfect circle. The choir stalls are unimaginably rich, the whole bible in little wooden figures trying to struggle out of the seats and panoplies. Of course there is cause to curse. There is such a glory in the choir as makes one sick at heart; 17th century cherubs and thunder clouds with shafts of gold thicker than any weaver's beam piercing them, and all sprawled in stucco right across the absidal arches. . . .

'Beauvais is all in height,' as the concierge said in its disparagement. . . . But we climbed all over it, and incomplete and faulty though it is there is something huger in the beauty of it than one can well describe. In the moonlight it was a perfect vision. . . . From Beauvais almost to Rouen in rain till the bykes were creaking and night closing in, so we stopped at a little inn, whose copper and brass pans and old chest and small, dried, aged, but motherly hostess you would like to draw, and the potage au lait more than made up for the *living* water we found in the ewer and which gave one unpleasant sensations when washing. Rouen is electric trams etc. We went to Croisset and saw Flaubert's lime walk. . . . his house is gone and his tulip tree, but there is still the little winding walk up the cliff and the little look-out summer house. . . . We also saw the Hotel Dieu of Rouen where he lived as a child and to whose lowest windows he and his sister used to climb up by vines to watch his father dissecting, and the same flies which settled on the corpses came buzzing out and settled on them and the flowers. . . . We rode up and down the rue

Flaubert, and in the Cathedral saw the St Julien window. . . . We were rather short of cash (in Dieppe) so we went to a very queer grub shop and got a rather strange glimpse of *low* life. Then we watched a Roundabout . . . quite altogether the Emperor of Roundabouts and in its way as decorated as a Cathedral, and French women in large skirts which filled out reminded one of Velasquez' Equestrian Queens. . . .

Far away

Travelling to distant places, recording them for a fascinated readership was stock in trade for topographical artists. Eventually this profession was to give way to photography, but when Edward Lear was in Corfu, the tide of commerce had not yet run out for him.

North Africa and the Near East had a romantic attraction for European artists. Morocco seemed to Delacroix to be an extraordinary land where he could rediscover the noble simplicity which had been lost in Europe since classical times. George Catlin had a similar feeling about the Indian peoples in America whom he hoped to record before what he saw as their inevitable doom overcame them.

The situation of Frederic Remington was rather different, a man travelling with the United States Army in a war, a role both exhilarating and exhausting.

Lear in Corfu

Edward Lear, author of limericks and the famous *Book of Nonsense* (1846) pursued a career as a travelling topographer. He published a series of books from various countries including Albania, Greece and Italy. One of his sites was Corfu which in his time was under British administration as a result of the peace settlement of 1815. In 1856 he was working on a panoramic view.[10]

9 October 1856

I trust to paint a magnificent large view of Corfu, straits and Albanian hills. This I trust to sell for 500£ as it will be my best, and is 9 feet long. If I can't sell it I shall instantly begin a picture 10 feet long and if that doesn't sell, one 12 feet long. Nothing like persisting in virtue.

Two years later he was working on two commissioned works.

10 January 1858

I shall begin a letter and let it burn up gradivally like the gun-powder which they throw on the fire. I have been working tooth and nail at Lord Clermont's Athos, & am succeeding in making it the best I have done of that 'oly mounting. In the foreground there is a Nilextree, which I take no ends of pains about, and the little woody dell will I think be a pet bit of the picture with Lord C. It is doubtless, though still to have much added, a better picture than the one I did at Redhouse, but I can't help that. The other 2, Mrs. Empson's Athos and Corfu, are also less good, which I am sorry for, but I can't help either, for naturally every successive piece of work should be better than its foregoer.

Lear left Corfu, but returned, and in 1863 had decided on an ambitious speculation, an exhibition to be held in Corfu town. Sir Henry Storks, the administrator of the Ionian islands, was one of his patrons, but he hoped for sales both to the English residents and the native inhabitants. Incidentally, there were plenty of knights around the islands, as a special order of knighthood had been created for the administration; the order of St Michael and St George only later became the customary British reward for diplomats.

1 March 1863

About the 20th I finished the last of 60 drawings – all of 10 or 12 guineas each in price – and last week the frames came, and then, after two days' insertion of the drawings, measuring and nail knocking, I have made a really remarkable gallery of watercolour works. This next week I have to ask some 70 or 80 sets of people to see this same gallery – but I doubt my success in selling the drawings. Cheap photographs are the order of the day now . . . Among those who most enjoy seeing what I have done, Sir H. Storks is eminent. His delight in looking over the drawings was very marked – and at once he bought one of Jerusalem and one of Corfu. Lady Wolff also examines everything minutely and with an eye evidently used to look at nature heartily. Others will irritate me – Sir C. Sargent to wit – who saw all 60 drawings in 19 minutes, calling over the names of each and saying '£700! why you must give a ball!' Fool! As yet I have sold £120 worth – but have not received one farthing – for great people generally suppose that artists gnaw their colours and brushes for food . . .

Delacroix in Morocco

North Africa had an allure in the 1830s, when Delacroix undertook his visit to Morocco. It was more adventurous curiosity than professional need which caused the artist to accept an invitation to join a diplomatic mission there; but he made good use of his opportunities. This letter describes a meeting with the emperor which formed the basis for a painting 'The Sultan of Morocco among his guards', shown at the Salon in 1845.

The status of this letter is that it was written for several people, although nominally addressed to J. B. Pierret; Delacroix expected it to be read by a circle of his close friends.

(to J. B. Pierret)[11] Meknes, 16 March, 1832

Yesterday we reached this town, the goal of our journey. We had taken ten days to cover fifty leagues. That seems nothing much. But it's nonetheless a tiring business when you jog along in the hot sun on uncomfortable saddles. How are you, my dear friends? Everything is tremendously African now. Our entry here was of the utmost beauty, and the sort of pleasure one may well hope to experience only once in one's life. All that happened to us that day was only the complement to what the journey had led us to expect. At every moment we were met by fresh armed tribes, who fired an extravagant amount of gunpowder in honour of our arrival. Each provincial governor passed us on to the next, whose guards came to augment our already sizable escort. From time to time we heard a few belated bullets whistling past in the midst of the rejoicings. We had, among other adventures, a river crossing, without bridges or boats, needless to say, which might be compared to the crossing of the Rhine, such was the quantity of rifle fire that greeted us. But all this was as nothing besides our reception in the capital. To begin with we were made to take the longest way in, so as to travel all round the city and appreciate its importance. The emperor had given orders for everyone to keep holiday and give us a festive welcome, under pain of the severest penalties, so that the crowds and the chaos were extreme. We knew that when the Austrians were welcomed here six months ago twelve men and fourteen horses were accidentally killed. Our small company thus had great difficulty in keeping together, and finding its bearings, amidst the thousands of rifle shots being fired in our faces. We were led in by a band of musicians and over twenty flags carried by men on horseback. The band was mounted, too; each horseman carried a kind of bagpipe round his neck, with a drum which he beat with two sticks, a large and small one, alternately and on either side. This made an extremely deafening din, mingled with the volleys of the cavalry and infantry and the enthusiasts who darted forth all around us to fire into our faces. We found it all infuriating and yet comical, and I look back on it now with less ill-temper. This triumphal entry, which resembled the ordeal of some wretched victims being led to the gallows, lasted from early morning until four in the afternoon. *Nota bene* that we had taken a light snack by way of breakfast at seven that morning in our tents. In the midst of my fury I noticed some very curious buildings in this town, in the Moorish style of course, but more impressive than those in Tangier.

20 March.

We have been held prisoner for the past five or six days in a house in the city, pending the time for our audience. As we are continually in one another's presence we are less inclined to gaiety and the hours seem very long, although the house we are in is a very curious specimen of Moorish architecture, which is that of all the palaces of Granada, of which you have seen engravings. But I am learning by experience that one's sensations are dulled in the course of time, and the picturesque stares you in the face so much all around that one ends by becoming insensitive to it. The day before yesterday we were brought a packet of letters by a messenger who travelled on foot from Tangier, since we have no means of communication in this country where there are no roads or bridges or boats on the rivers. My heart beat faster at the thought that there might be something for me: but you're all unkind to me, and yet I swear to you that a word from one or other of you would have delighted me more than the whole of Africa.

I imagine we shall have to stay here another ten days or so. I shall write to you from Tangier to tell you that I am likely to return. All my love to your and yours. I still love you, despite your silence.

23 March

Yesterday we were received by the emperor. He granted us a favour which he never grants to anybody, that of visiting his private apartments and his gardens. It is all exceedingly curious. He receives his visitors on horseback, with all his guard around him on foot. He suddenly appears through a doorway and comes towards you, with a parasol behind him. He's a rather handsome man. He looks very like our own king, only with a beard and somewhat younger. He was followed by his state coach, a sort of wheelbarrow drawn by a mule. So I've reached the goal of my journey. Our main concern now is not to moulder away too long in Africa. I'm afraid we may be held up some time in Tangier. All my fellow travellers have been getting letters. I'm the only one who has had none from anybody. I'm not really surprised at not receiving any through the ministry of Foreign Affairs, as they have not written yet, but I reckon you must long before this have received the letter in which I begged you to write to me through Piron; since, despite my hopes, it's still extremely uncertain when I shall return, write to me up to the last moment, and in case Piron should not have received the letter in which I gave him the requisite address, please be kind enough to give him your letters, telling him to address them to M. Thibandier, French consular agent at Gibraltar, to be sent to M. Delacroix at Tangier. The slightest details are precious to an exile; when I say news, I don't mean political or literary news but your own, the simplest things, how Felix is, and Pierret's wife and children, whatever you like, words and lines in your handwriting which, received here in Africa, would be very precious to me. Please remember me to all our friends. Although I'm on excellent terms with my two fellow travellers I miss being able to talk about any of you with them. Well, pray heaven not to drag out my exile too long, and in any case, write. Farewell, farewell.

Eugène.

Felix, give news of me to Henry.

This letter is for him as well. Tell him to remember me to M. and Mme. Destandis.

Pierret, please, when you go to my studio, loosen the spring of the easel on which 'The Battle of Nancy' is standing, so as to lessen the strain on it, and let the weight of the picture bear on its base: it's a bit late, but no matter. All my love to our friends. Write, please, write. Post this letter to Mme. Dalton. Let her know about it when you have a chance.

Roberts reaches Egypt

Another traveller to North Africa was the topographical artist David Roberts, who had none of the diplomatic advantages of Delacroix. His arrival in Alexandria is described in a letter to his daughter Christine; his powers of close observations are as evident in his writing as in the reliable detail which make so attractive a feature of his lithographic drawings.

(to Christine Roberts)[12] Alexandria, 24 September 1838

My dear Christine, – I am delighted to inform you that after a delightful voyage I am here safe and sound in Egypt. I left Marseilles in the steamer, the 'Dante' on the 11th, and encountered much stormy weather until we reached Civita Vecchia, where I first set foot on the shore of Italy, which was rather tantalising, as we were within two hours' journey of the Eternal City. We continued our passage amid delightful weather to Malta, and I was much pleased with the city of Valetta and its immense fortifications, which seem in dimensions to exceed Gibraltar. We changed steamers here, and proceeded to Lyra, a small island in the Greek archipelago. The ancient city crowns a hill, on the summit of which there is a Greek convent. I landed and ascended the eminence and was amply rewarded for my exertions. On the right lay the island of Delos, and, stretching far away in the ocean, Crete, or as it is now called Candia. We changed vessels here, and the ship which we now went aboard was crowded with pilgrims from Constantinople on their way to Mecca: Turks of very varied costume – men, women, and children – carrying with them luggage and provision for their passage through the desert. They were all deck passengers, and I never saw such a picturesque assemblage. Of course my sketch-book and I were busily employed. They prostrated themselves and prayed five or six time a-day, which was a most impressive sight. This morning we were all early astir, and Alexandria lay before us, its mosques and palm-trees giving it a different character from anything I had seen; while immediately over it rose the remains of the ancient city, now a mass of rubbish, but which at one time contained a population of 600,000 inhabitants. In the bay were numerous ships, many of them vessels of war. Our ship was soon surrounded by the most picturesque boatmen in the world, pulling, hauling, and bawling – each fighting for which should have the passengers.

On landing from the boats the scene was still more exciting: such scrambling among the poor black porters to get hold of the luggage, that it was with great difficulty you could keep it under your eye; and they submitted to be kicked and buffeted, all for the sake of a few halfpence. On entering the city we saw long trains of loaded camels and donkeys; Turks in rich dresses; negroes, some nude; with Greeks, Jews and people of all nations. Having taken up our abode, we sallied forth to see the lions, visited the bazaars and the slave market, the latter peculiarly disgusting. The slaves were mostly girls: some from Circassia were well dressed: others, negroes, squatted on the ground, with scanty bits of matting thrown around them, and in a sun that would have killed a European. It was altogether a sickening sight, and I left it proud that I belonged to a nation who had abolished slavery. In the evening, having procured guides and donkeys, we proceeded to the ancient city. We passed through a burial ground, where a few poor Turks were scooping a shallow grave in the sand. The corpse, wrapped up in an old brown covering, lay on a sort of barrow, and half-a-dozen women were wailing. One, in particular, seemed overpowered by grief: she had on her knees an infant, apparently about two years of age. Immediately over this rose Pompey's Pillar, with which I was somewhat disappointed. Afterwards rode to see Cleopatra's Needle.

25th. I have been again over the ruins of the old city, and, with the exception of the portico of a Roman temple, half excavated, saw little beyond what I had seen yesterday. The expense of laying the whole of this temple open would be trifling, the price of labour is so low; the work is generally done by girls at about 2d. a day. There is a double row of granite columns, and on the walls are Roman paintings.

I have met with the greatest kindness here. To-day I dine with

Mr. Thorburn, the consul, and to-morrow with Colonel Campbell, who is indefatigable in his endeavours to serve me, and has given me a letter of introduction to Mehemet Ali.

I suppose you are inhaling the sea-breezes. Remember me kindly to Mr. Cooke, Edward and the young ladies.

David Roberts.

Catlin records noble races

One incentive for travel was to record sights which few people had seen. In the case of George Catlin this motive was complemented by a sense of history; he knew he was recording what would soon be destroyed, never to be seen again.

Topography is too modest a word to describe his ambitious programme; for he worked on the scale of a scientific or geographical expedition, and he left an irreplaceable legacy. The extract is from one of the letters Catlin published in 1841.[13]

Mouth of the Yellowstone River, 1832

I arrived at this place yesterday in the steamer *Yellow Stone*, after a voyage of nearly three months from St. Louis, a distance of two thousand miles, the greater part of which has never before been navigated by steam; and the almost insurmountable difficulties which continually oppose the *voyageur* on this turbid stream, have been by degrees overcome by the indefatigable zeal of Mr. Chouteau, a gentleman of great perseverence, and part proprietor of the boat. To the politeness of this gentleman I am indebted for my passage from St. Louis to this place, and I had also the pleasure of his *company*, with that of Major Sanford, the government agent for the Missouri Indians . . .

You will, no doubt, be somewhat surprised on the receipt of a letter from me, so far strayed into the Western World; and still more startled, when I tell you that I am here in the full enthusiasm and practice of my art. That enthusiasm alone has brought me into this remote region, 3,500 miles from my native soil; the last 2,000 of which have furnished me with almost limitless models, both in landscape and the human figure, exactly suited to my feelings. I am now in the full possession and enyoyments of those conditions, on which alone I was induced to pursue the art as a profession; and in anticipation of which alone, my admiration for the art could ever have been kindled into a pure flame. I mean the free use of nature's undisguised models, with the privilege of selecting for myself. If I am here losing the benefit of the fleeting fashions of the day, and neglecting that elegant polish, which the world says an artist should draw from a continual intercourse with the polite world; yet have I this consolation, that in this country, I am entirely divested of those dangerous steps and allurements which beset an artist in fashionable life; and have little to steal my thoughts away from the contemplation of the beautiful models that are about me. If, also, I have not here the benefit of that feeling of emulation, which is the life and the spur to the arts, where artists are associates together; yet am I surrounded by living models of such elegance and beauty, that I feel an unceasing excitement of a much higher order – the certainty that I am drawing knowledge from the true source. My enthusiastic admiration of man in the honest and elegant simplicity of nature has always fed the warmest feelings of my bosom, and shut half the avenues to my heart against the specious refinements of the accomplished world. This feeling, together with the desire to study my art, independently of the embarrassments which the ridiculous fashions of civilized society have thrown in its way, has led me to the wilderness for a while, as the true school of the arts.

I have for a long time been of the opinion, that the wilderness of our country afforded models equal to those from which the Grecian sculptors transferred to the marble such inimitable grace and beauty; and I am now more confirmed in this opinion, since I have immersed myself in the midst of thousands and tens of thousands of these knights of the forest; whose whole lives are lives of chivalry, and whose daily feats, with their naked limbs, might vie with those of the Grecian youths in the beautiful rivalry of the Olympic games.

No man's imagination, with all the aids of description that can be given to it, can ever picture the beauty and wildness of scenes that may be daily witnessed in this romantic country; of hundreds of these graceful youths, without a care to wrinkle or a fear to disturb the full expression of pleasure and enjoyment that beams upon their faces – their long black hair mingling with their horses' tails, floating in the wind, while they are flying over the carpeted prairie, and dealing death with their spears and arrows, to a band of infuriated buffaloes; or their splendid procession in a war-parade, arrayed in all their gorgeous colors and trappings, moving with most exquisite grace and manly beauty, added to that bold defiance which man carries on his front, who acknowledges no superior on earth, and who is amenable to no laws except the laws of God and honor.

In addition to the knowledge of human nature and my art, which I hope to acquire by this toilsome and expensive undertaking, I have another in view, which, if it should not be of equal service to me, will be of no less interest and value to posterity. I have, for many years past, contemplated the noble races of red men who are now spread over these trackless forests and boundless prairies, melting away at the approach of civilization. Their rights invaded, their morals corrupted, their lands wrested from them, their customs changed, and therefore lost to the world; and they at last sunk into the earth, and the ploughshare turning the sod over their graves, and I have flown to their rescue – not of their lives or of their race (for they are '*doomed*' and must perish), but to the rescue of their looks and their modes, at which the acquisitive world may hurl their poison and every besom of destruction, and trample them down and crush them to death; yet, phoenix-like, they may rise from the 'stain on the painter's palette', and live again upon canvas, and stand forth for centuries yet to come, the living monuments of a noble race. For this purpose, I have designed to visit every tribe of Indians on the Continent, if my life should be spared; for the purpose of procuring portraits of distinguished Indians, of both sexes in each tribe, painted in their native costume; accompanied with pictures of their villages, domestic habits, games, mysteries, religious ceremonies, and so forth with anecdotes, traditions, and history of their respective nations.

If I should live to accomplish my design, the result of my labors will doubtless be interesting to future ages; who will have little else left from which to judge of the original inhabitants of this simple race of beings, who require but a few years more of the march of civilization and death, to deprive them of all their native customs and character. I have been kindly supplied by the Commander-in-Chief of the Army and the Secretary of War, with letters to the commander of every military post, and every Indian agent on the Western Frontier, with instructions to render me all the facilities in their power, which will be of great service to me in so arduous an undertaking. The opportunity afforded me by familiarity with so many tribes of human beings in the simplicity of nature, devoid of the deformities of art; of drawing fair conclusions in the interesting sciences of physiognomy and phrenology; of manner and customs, rites, ceremonies, and the like; and the opportunity of examining the geology and mineralogy of this western, and yet unexplored country, will enable me occasionally to entertain you with much new and interesting information, which I shall take equal pleasure in communication by an occasional Letter in my clumsy way.

Remington rides with the army

The name of Frederic Remington breathes adventure, associated as it is with American Indians, the United States cavalry, war in Cuba, horses and cowboys.

Remington's vivid reportage of the West is part of legend, whether in paintings or bronze. Some of his letters echo his action-packed reputation. We can start with a letter from Indian country to his wife.

(to Eva Remington)[14]

Tenth U.S. Cavalry
Fort Grant
June 22 (1888)

My dear girl: – We just returned this afternoon from a two weeks scout up as far as the Perial mountains. The particulars are so numerous as to furnish new material for many pictures. We 'pulled out' of Grant with four men, a Sargeant – Clark – two packers and four pack mules – myself on a company horse – the first days march was through the Taylor canyon of the Sierra Benitos – it was tough – the toughest thing I ever went through except our passage of the Mescal range later on – the rocks often gave bad footing – we dismounted and led our horses. The air was rare and grew rarer as we ascended – I puffed like a tug boat. – I felt like dropping in my tracks at times – We got off the trail – Clark and 2 men – on the Knife like ridge of the divide we could look over the Sulphur Spring valley and the Gila valley at the same point – with the blue mass of the mountains towering on every side. It was grand but it did not repay the torture of the ascent. Well we camped – saw a wild bull fight – the next day I was very sore – we marched about 30 miles across [?] and wastes, cactus and alkali – the water nearly boiled in the canteen if it had not been for my helmet I could not have stood it. – Well I see I cannot describe it all but we made Fort Thomas and on to the San Carlos Agency. There I saw the ration day Apaches by the thousand and black soldiers until you cant rest. – a Chinaman ran the officers mess – four races of people in one group – quite a commentary on America – it is awfully hot in the Gilas Valley – the water is all luke warm that we drink.

We then went on to the Perial range under the guidance of Lieut. Watson of the '10th Nubian Horse' – we here saw mountain scenery which was too grand to describe – we came back there over another trail, lost it and made plumb over the tip top of the Mescal range – that day and the next – ride through the Gila valley – with the sun scorching and the dust rising in a solid column clear out of sight in the sky made an experience which I will never forget. I have lost 20 pounds at least – feel well and am perfectly blistered in the face – the skin is coming off but I will soon be all right to give you an idea of how hot the first Gila valley day was I will say that the three greyhounds that Clark took gave out laid down and were abandoned – I took lots of instantaneous shots – don't know what they will be – You must not write here any more – I leave here Tuesday for Fort Sill Indian Territory. I dont know how long I will be there or where I will go so that I dont see as you can write anywhere until you hear from me again. I will certainly be home before 1st August and will probably come before – I am very anxious to see you in fact I cannot stay away as long as I should –

It is a very successful trip and will help me professionally very greatly – the photo of you and the baby was very good especially the three quarter length.

Well good bye little girl when I come home we will put up a job and have some fun – I am tired have been in the saddle all day and cant keep awake any longer. Do not pay 24 on the London drawing – I dont want it – it should come through for nothing – or have it destroyed – presume Kemble can fix that – if he cant let it lay

Love and kisses from
Your
Fred

There is a celebrated story about Remington as a newspaper artist, when he was sent by William Randolph Hearst to Cuba in a troubled time. The two are said to have exchanged the following telegrams:

(Remington to Hearst)
Everything is quiet. There is no trouble. There will be no war. I wish to return.

(Hearst to Remington)
Please remain. You furnish the picture and I'll furnish the war.

A Remington bronze of horse and rider was bought to present to Colonel Theodore Roosevelt by his regiment, to the pleasure of both the sculptor and the Colonel.

(to Colonel Roosevelt)

Endion
New Rochester
[September 1898]

My dear Colonel Roosevelt – what can give the blood a stronger action than when the whole tribe says 'Ha' – ? you know – you have felt it: –

And what is next – is the sensation, when the tribe says 'aye' – I have felt this –

The greatest compliment I ever had or ever can have was when the Rough Riders put their brand upon my bronze.

After this everything will be mere fuss – I am

Yours faithfully
Frederic Remington

(to Frederic Remington, dictated)

Oyster bay, Long Island
September 19, 1898

Frederic Remington Esq.,
New Rochelle. N.Y.
My dear Remington: – I think your letter pleased the rough riders who saw it, as much as their action pleased you. It was the most appropriate gift the Regiment could possibly have given me, and the one I would have valued most. I have looked hungrily at that bronze, but to have it come to me in this precise way, seemed almost too good.

Faithfully yours,
Theodore Roosevelt

8

AFTERWORD

We have seen how varied the careers of artists through the nineteenth century could be, and some of the evidence that their letters can provide. This last chapter provides a medley of correspondence, some letters documenting final years, including a little about honours and reputation, and something too about melancholy topics.

The century did not see many artists living to a great age, though Goya was an octogenarian, and both Trumbull and Watts lived to be 86. Many of our artists died in their sixties, rather fewer in their seventies. Some artists may be thought to have died before their time – Courbet, for example, whose enemies made his last years hard to bear, and who died at 58. Of those who died in their thirties and forties, Géricault, Holl, Rethel, and Seurat are representatives, while of those who died younger, Marie Bashkirtseff was one of the century's many victims of tuberculosis at the age of 23.

Suicide, a different sort of premature death, makes its grim appearance in these pages. Benjamin Haydon, several of whose letters have been quoted, has a memorial in his last note to his wife. He wrote it before shooting himself in his studio in front of one of those historical canvases which he had hoped in vain would ensure his fame and prosperity.[1]

> God bless thee, dearest love! Pardon thy last pang! God bless thee in thy dear widowhood: I hope Sir Robert will consider I have earned a pension for thee. A thousand kisses – Thy dear husband – and love to the last.
>
> B R Haydon

There were other sombre ends to artists' lives in an age when medicine had less to offer than more recently, or the force of circumstances gave an unexpected twist, say exile, to a career. On the other hand, there were also last years for some artists of comfort and distinction, friendship and support.

Latter days

Letters from some artists speak of the conditions or the moods of later years, including several which document unexpected turns of fortune.

Delacroix is no longer carefree
This letter was written when Delacroix was 52, but it is tinged with a melancholy that might be more readily expected in an older man.

(to Charles Raymond Soulier)[2] Paris 23 March 1850

Dear friend,
I was sorry not to have been at home when your dear boy called and left your letter. I was very glad to have news of you, although your letter was sad on account of your son's departure. Life is just a series of shocks, and they are nearly always sorrows. The times we live in provide a fuller measure of these than life normally entails. The present causes grief, the future anxiety; only the past remains, and to take refuge in memory is a great consolation. Where is our carefree life now? I never cross the Place Vendôme without looking up at the little window which is still the same; but how many things, or rather how many men have changed, not to speak of all that has vanished! A month or two ago I was shown the paintings of animals that I did at Beffes, some four-and-twenty years ago! The poor marquis having died

in his turn, his picture was for sale. We all end up at the second-hand dealer's; that's the universal burial ground. Work is my surest refuge, not only against *ennui* but against sorrow, and I know you too appreciate this authentic solace. Look after yourself, for we must still care for our bodies first of all. Your son Paul is delightful. This is the younger generation that must take our place. These gloomy thoughts of ours don't enter into their young heads, and so much the better. Are you coming here soon? Pierret was unable to tell me.

Goodbye, with all my love. Eug. Delacroix

Lear follows a strict regime

Towards the end of his life Edward Lear suffered from increased ill-health; his concerned friends made sure that in his retirement he had a comfortable Italian home at San Remo. They went further. When a building was put up so close to his home that it obscured his view, his friends ensured he was able to build a new house.

Lear's visitors in Italy included rich friends like Lord Northbrook, one of his patrons, with his daughter Emma. The following letter describes the pattern of the artist's later life, written in the year before he died.[3]

April 1, 1887

You will be glad to know that I go on improving. I have walked out on the Terrace, (always helped of course,) and have been more able to balance myself than I was a week ago. This is my unvaried scheme of diet. 6 A.M. cup of black coffee. 9 A.M. two eggs unbeaten with sugar, and then diluted with tea: two pieces of dry toast, and a thin slice of brown bread with butter. 10.45, a ¾ glass of Port wine and a biscuit. 1 P.M. lunch, generally fish or brains or some light food, and nothing more unless indigestion pains in left side worry, when I take ¼ glass of cognac and water. 7.15 P.M. bed, which I am undressed for and put into. I regret to say my good servant Achille San Pietro who succeeded Luigi Russoni, goes today. His silly wife at Como would not let him stay, professing to believe that all Sanseno was full of earthquake, whereas nothing has happened *here* though horrors enough at villages around.

Northbrook's stay and Lady Emma's were a very great blessing and I wish them back hourly . . .

Courbet appeals for help

Gustave Courbet was at the high tide of his fortune in 1870. Indeed, when he was offered the Légion d'Honneur, he refused it disdainfully. This is how he wrote to his family.

I am overwhelmed with compliments. I received three hundred letters with such compliments as nobody in the world ever received. Everyone agrees that I am the foremost man in France. M. Thiers summoned me to his home to compliment me. I even receive princesses to the same end, and a dinner for eighty or a hundred was given to congratulate me. The entire press and all the scholars of Paris were there. When I go down the street I have to keep my hat in my hand, like a priest.

But his triumph had a short life. For his part in the Commune, Courbet was put into prison. Nor was that the end of his misfortunes. He was sentenced to crippling fines, impossible to pay, for the re-erection of the Vendôme Column, pulled down by the Communards, an act for which he was held responsible.

In the year of his death he wrote from his exile in Switzerland to Whistler, explained his situation and asked for help.

(to James A McNeill Whistler)[4]

Tour-de-Peilz, Canton Vaud February 14, 1877

My dear Whistler:

It is quite a while since we last saw each other. It is a pity, for our ideas have changed. Where is the time, my friend, when we were happy and with no other cares but those of art. Do you remember Trouville and Jo who clowned around to amuse us? In the evening she used to sing Irish songs so beautifully, she had a feeling and talent for art. I also remember our stealthy move from the Casino to the Hôtel de la Mer, where we went bathing on a frozen beach, and the salad bowls full of shrimp with fresh butter, not to mention the cutlet at lunch, which allowed us to paint the sky, the sea, and the fish all the way to the horizon. And our payment consisted of dreams and sky.

I still have the *Portrait of Jo* which I will never sell. Everyone admires it. The painting of the *Misses Potter* has been bought by Durand-Ruel and must have gone to London. It is very surprising that M. Potter did not buy it; it is strange, try to find it. I was never paid for it. Durand-Ruel has stopped his payments especially where I am concerned. He behaved like everyone else. Everything has been stolen from me, and my life has been destroyed.

What years of misfortunes, what torments, what suffering, what cruelties, how many prisons! How many times have I escaped death and the clutches of those cannibals. They have dragged me through the streets with my wrists in chains, they have locked me in dungeons without air, etc., etc. It is impossible to tell it all.

Let's turn to something else: I am in a charming countryside – the most beautiful in the world – by Lake Geneva, which is surrounded by gigantic mountains. You would like the sky, for on one side is the lake and its horizon. It is better than Trouville, because of the landscape.

I will be sentenced one of these days to pay for the Vendôme Column: 333,000 francs, ten thousand francs a year from painting. So I have to squeeze ten thousand francs a year from painting. At the moment I would like you to lend me a hand. Your friend M. Bergeron did not want me to send a painting of a *Calf* and [still life of] *Apples*, which are at this moment at M. Deschamps's, I believe. He was positive that I could sell them in London without sending them to Philadelphia, and in a letter I have here he has engaged to do it. Go and see about it, if you please, for the price of eight thousand francs has been offered to the Genoese merchant Pia, who represents M. Bergeron. Also go and see M. Gillman, 14 Ashley Place, S.W., and Edmond Levrand, likewise a friend of M. Bergeron, at 93 Great Titchfield Street/Oxford Street. I have entrusted M. B. Reitlinger of Vienna, Austria, with four paintings for the Philadelphia Exhibition, which I believe have been lost. Not only that, they are already asking me four hundred dollars, and I have paid the costs already. With regard to that, see Messrs. Grünebaum, Ballin & Co., Angel Court, Throgmorton Street. Ask them about Reitlinger.

Well, my friend, that is quite a bit of work for you.

Yours sincerely, please answer me. G. Courbet

Bartolozzi pines in Lisbon
Francesco Bartolozzi also became an exile but in rather different circumstances; he had made his reputation in London as an engraver, where he was a founder member of the Royal Academy, but dealers did not continue to supply him with work. At the age of 75 he accepted a pension from the Prince Regent of Portugal. His exile was unhappy, and he was to die without seeing London again.[5]

May 1814

Here at present we are destitute of every requisite in our profession – gravers, varnish, tracing paper, and black for printing, all are very dear and very bad. I have engraved one of the views of Lisbon; the copper furnished me resembled lead; so that with a bad drawing and worse copper I have made a wretched thing of it. Thus is an artist sacrificed.

I was in hopes last summer of seeing London once more, though I had no expectation of obtaining employment, especially as you have so many eminent men in our profession. Some of the dealers, you well know, have made fortunes by my poor works – but now there is no fortune to be made . . . My good Prince here affords me a maintenance, but I would nevertheless have sacrificed everything with pleasure to revisit that country to which I owe a debt of gratitude for the benefits I have received from it that will never be erased from my memory.

Goya in Bordeaux
Francisco Goya also died abroad, at the age of 82. Before writing this letter, he had made a brief visit to Paris where the Duchess of San Fernando lived at this time, but he returned to winter in Bordeaux. His situation was unusual, for although he was officially in the employment of the Spanish court, his work was not in demand. The touch of a practised courtier can be seen, though, in his witty compliment of a gift of drawings to a patron.

(to the Duchess of San Fernando)[6] Nov 30, 1824, Bordeaux

Dear and most respected lady: when I left Paris to come here, I arranged the journey in a great hurry: time was short, I had no money and I accepted the offer of some friends who advanced the expenses of the journey. I had only a few hours left and I gave orders for a farewell card to be sent to your Grace's house: had all this not occurred, I should not have failed to request the honour of presenting myself to his Grace and yourself.

Here I am then, without knowing what I should do with myself. I have requested an extension, if only to pass the winter in the warmth of the fireside, and I do not know whether his Majesty will see fit to grant it.

I am taking the liberty of sending your Grace these three commission-bearers, whom I have especially charged with assuring you how grateful I am that you should remember me and how much I desire to please and serve you. They are three drawings who presented themselves at the fair of Bordeaux two months ago, and I thought it a good idea to take a sketch of their faces and their little figures. The one in pantaloons is 28 inches tall, while of the other two (who are husband and wife) she is 21 inches tall and her husband 20. I shall be very pleased if they carry out this commission, as is the desire of the invalid who sends them.

With this I repeat myself at the disposal of your Grace, as also of his Grace the Duke: wishing you both the greatest of happiness.

Vita brevis

David refuses to return to Paris

The career of Jacques-Louis David was spectacular and dramatic, leading as it did from success under the *ancien régime*, through the years of the revolution during which the artist voted for Louis XVI's execution, to the era of Napoleon, whose favoured painter he became. He was accepted by the Bourbon regime, but on Napoleon's return from Elba he returned to his former allegiance. The Emperor visited him on 16 April at Cluny, and David became his First Painter again, a Commander of the Légion d'Honneur, and despite little faith in Napoleon's chances of regaining power, he signed an Addendum to the Constitution including universal suffrage. At Napoleon's defeat and final exile, David was subject to fierce retribution. This was the wording of Article 7, passed on January 16, 1816.[7]

Any regicides who, in spite of almost boundless leniency, voted for the Addendum and accepted work or offices from the usurper, thereby declaring themselves irreconcilable enemies of France, shall be banished from the kingdom for ever and must leave it within a month . . .

David chose exile in Brussels, where he was highly esteemed, and where he was both to die and be buried. This is how he described his refusal to return to Paris.

(to his son)[7] Jan 1, 1819

All my colleagues are going back to France, and I should certainly go with them if I were weak enough to ask for my recall in writing. You know how proud your father is – could he do something like that? I was old enough to know what I was doing, I didn't act on impulse. Time will reveal the truth. In this country people who believe in uprightness and integrity respect me . . . I'm valued in this country where I live, and I've turned down a great king who wanted me to organise a ministry in his Prussian states. I can rest here, my conscience is clear, what more do I need?

A letter of consolation

Antoine Jean Gros remained a loyal friend to David after the latter's exile to Belgium and sought to promote his interests, even at the expense of his own position under the rule of Louis XVII, from whom he had accepted a barony. He was deeply upset by David's death, and tried in vain to enable David's body to be returned to Paris for burial. Permission was refused, and the funeral took place in Brussels. This letter of consolation was written to one of David's two sons.[8]

Sir, and my dear friend,
I can address you thus since at this sad moment it is forty years ago that I received my first lessons from your celebrated father, and I saw you, for the first time, you and your brother, so young, playing around me.

I have feared every day to learn of the death of this great man, so much has the decline he has suffered prepared us for it. It is meanwhile a consolation to know that love of his art had so invaded all his thoughts that it became, according to your brother's noble expression, a triumph of the soul over the sufferings of the body.

In him, in him alone, the French School was lifted up to the heights of the most beautiful days of Pericles. May the study of masterpieces of art and the recall of the great doctrines which he has left us save us from the decadence with which so great a loss threatens us.

Students from the art schools have placed on your mother's knee the crown and crêpe with which they hope to be able to attach to his masterpieces.

I join my thanks to yours for the hospitable city which honours him and is proud to possess the ashes of such a great man. Fifty-five years of fame among his fellow citizens, an immortality to which one cannot (place bounds), such will be for ever the name of David in this France whose art he raised to the height of the finest centuries of Greece.

Please present my respectful homage to your ladies. I have no need to assure you again how much I share your great sadness.

Accept, my dear sir and dear friend, renewed assurance of my best wishes etc

Baron Gros

Mourning for Manet

Berthe Morisot here writes to her sister about the death of her brother-in-law Edouard Manet in 1883.

(to Edma)[9]

My dear Edma, thank you for your affectionate letter, and thanks also to Adolphe, who wrote Eugène a note that touched him very much. These last days were very painful; poor Edouard suffered atrociously. His agony was horrible. In a word, it was death in one of its most appalling forms that I once again witnessed at very close range.

If you add to these almost physical emotions my old bonds of friendship with Edouard, an entire past of youth and work suddenly ending, you will understand that I am crushed. The expressions of sympathy have been intense and universal; his richly endowed nature compelled everyone's friendship; he also had an intellectual charm, a warmth, something indefinable, so that, on the day of his funeral, all the people who came to attend – and who are usually so indifferent on such occasions – seemed to me like one big family mourning one of their own.

I shall never forget the days of my friendship and intimacy with him, when I sat for him and when the charm of his mind kept me alert during those long hours.

Van Gogh writes from an asylum

The outstanding letters written by Vincent van Gogh to his brother touch on all sorts of subjects besides his art. This letter exemplifies that range, while being also a poignant reminder of personal courage in sad circumstances.

(to Theo van Gogh)[10] St Rémy, May 25, 1889

My dear Theo,

The letter I have just received from you gives me great pleasure. You tell me that J. H. Weissenbruch has two pictures at the exhibitions – but I imagined he was dead – am I wrong? Certainly he's a mighty good artist and a decent big-hearted fellow.

What you say about the 'Woman Rocking' pleases me; it is very true that the common people, who are content with chromos and melt when they hear a barrel organ, are in some vague way right, perhaps more sincere than certain men about town who go to the Salon.

Gauguin, if he will accept it, give him the copy of the 'Woman Rocking' which was not mounted on a stretcher, and another to Bernard as a token of friendship. But if Gauguin wants the sunflowers it is only perfectly fair that he should give you in exchange something you like equally well.

Gauguin himself liked the sunflowers better later on when he had been looking at them a good while.

You must realize that if you arrange them this way, say the 'Woman Rocking' in the middle and the two canvases of sunflowers to right and left, it makes a sort of triptych.

And then the yellow and orange tones of the head will gain more brilliance by the proximity of the yellow wings.

And then you will understand what I wrote you, that my idea had been to make a decoration as it might be for instance for the end of the cabin of a ship. Then, as the size increases, the summary workmanship is justified. The frame for the centre is the red one. And the two sunflowers which go with it, are the ones framed in narrow strips.

You see that this frame of plain laths does quite well, and a frame like this one costs only very little. It would perhaps be a good thing to frame the red and green vineyards that way, the 'Sower' and the 'Furrows' and the bedroom interior as well.

Here is a new canvas of 30, once again as ordinary as a chromo in the little shops, which represents the eternal nests of greenery for lovers.

Some thick tree trunks covered with ivy, the ground also covered with ivy and periwinkle, a stone bench and a bush of roses pale in the cold shadow. In the foreground some plants with a white calix. It is green, violet and rose.

The problem – which unfortunately is lacking in the chromos of the little shops and the barrel organs – is to get some distinction into it.

Since I have been here, the deserted garden, planted with large pines beneath which grows the grass, tall and unkempt and mixed with various weeds, has sufficed for my work and I have not yet gone outside. However the country round St. Rémy is very beautiful and bit by bit I shall go and stay at places probably.

But by staying here, the doctor will naturally be better able to see what is wrong and will be, I hope, more reassured as to my being allowed to paint.

I *assure* you I am quite all right here and that temporarily I see no reason at all for coming to board in Paris or near it. I have a little room with greenish grey paper with two curtains of sea-green with a design of very pale roses, brightened by slight touches of blood-red.

These curtains, probably the relics of some rich and ruined defunct, are very pretty in design. From the same source probably comes a very worn armchair, recovered with an upholstery splashed like a Diaz or a Monticelli, with brown, red, rose, white, cream, black, forget-me-not blue and bottle green. Through the iron-barred window I see a square of corn in an enclosure, a perspective like Van Goyen, above which I see in the morning the sun rising in his glory. As well as this – as there are more than 30 rooms empty – I have another as well to work in.

The food is so so. It tastes naturally rather mouldy, like in a shoddy restaurant in Paris or a boarding house. As these poor souls do absolutely nothing (not a book, nothing to distract them but a game of bowls and a game of draughts) they have no other daily distraction than to stuff themselves with chick peas, haricots, lentils, and other groceries and provisions from the colonies in set quantities and at set hours.

As the digestion of these objects offers certain difficulties, they fill their days thus in a way as inoffensive as it is cheap.

But without joking, the *fear* of madness is leaving me a good deal, as I see at close quarters those who are affected by it, as in the future I may very easily be.

Formerly I felt repulsion for these creatures, and it was a harrowing thought for me to reflect that many of our profession, Troyon, Marchal, Méryon, Jundt, M. Maris, Monticelli and heaps more had ended like this. I could not bring myself even to picture them in that condition. Well, now I think of all this without fear, that is to say I find it no more frightful than if these people had been stricken with something else, phthisis or syphilis for instance. These artists, I see them take on again their old serenity, and is it a little thing, I ask you, to recover again the ancients of our profession? That without joking is a thing I am profoundly thankful for.

For though there are some who howl or rave continually there is much real friendship here one for another, they say, we must put up with others so that others will put up with us, and other very sound arguments, which they put into practice thus. And between ourselves we understand each other very well. I can for instance sometimes chat with one of them who can only answer in incoherent sounds, because he is not afraid of me.

If someone has an attack the others look after him and interfere so that he does himself no harm.

The same for those whose mania it is to fly often into rages. The old inhabitants, if combat there is. . . .

It is true there are some whose condition is more serious, who are either dirty or dangerous. These are in another courtyard. I am having a bath now twice a week and stay in it two hours, my stomach is infinitely better than it was a year ago, so as far as I know I have only to go on. Besides I shall spend less here I think, reckoning I have work again here on the stocks, for the scenery is lovely.

My hope would be that at the end of a year I shall know better what I can do and what I want to do better than now. Then little by little the idea of a fresh start will come to me. To come back to Paris or anywhere at all in no way takes my fancy. I think my place is here. Extreme enervation is, in my opinion, what most of those suffer from who have been here for years. Now my work will in a certain measure preserve me from that.

The room where we stay on wet days is like a third class waiting room in some dead-alive village, the more so as there are some distinguished lunatics who always wear a hat, spectacles, and cane, and travelling cloak, like at a bathing resort almost, and they represent the passengers.

I am forced to ask you again for some paints and especially for canvas. When I send you the four canvases of the garden I have in hand, you will see that considering life is spent mostly in the garden, it is not so unhappy. Yesterday I drew a very big, rather rare night moth, called the death's head, its colouring of amazing distinction, black, grey, cloudy white tinged with carmine or shading indistinctly to olive green; it is very big. To paint it I had to kill it and it was a pity, the beastie was so beautiful. I will send you the drawing with some other drawings of plants.

You could take off the stretchers from the canvases at Tanguy's or at your place, which have dried enough, and then put on to the stretchers any new ones that you think worth it. Gauguin ought to be able to tell you the address of a man who could reline the canvas of 'The Bedroom,' and not too dear. That, *I imagine*, ought to be repaired for 5 francs; if it is more, then don't have it done. I do not think Gauguin paid more when he had his own canvases relined pretty often, or Cézanne's, or Pissarro's.

I am again – speaking of my condition – so grateful for another thing. I gather from others that they also have heard in their attacks strange sounds and voices as I did, and that to their eyes too things seemed to be changing. And that lessens the horror that I retained at first of the attack I have had, and which when it comes on you unawares cannot but frighten you beyond measure. Once you know that it is part of the disease, you take it like anything else. If it had not been that I have seen other lunatics close to, I should not have been able to free myself from constantly dwelling upon it. For the anguish and suffering are no joke once you are caught by an attack. Most epileptics bit their tongue and wound themselves. Rey told me that he had seen a case where someone had wounded himself like me in the ear, and I think I heard a doctor here say, when he came to see me with the superintendant, that he also had seen it before. I really think that once you know what it is, once you are conscious of your condition and of being subject to attacks, that then you can do something yourself not to be taken aback by the suffering or the terror. Now for five months it has been going on lessening I have good hope of getting over it, or at least of not having attacks of such violence. There is someone here who has been shouting and talking like me *all the time* for a fortnight, he thinks he hears voices and words in the echoes of the corridors, probably because the nerves of the ear are diseased and too sensitive, and in my case it was sight and hearing at once, which according to what Rey told me one day is usual in the beginning of epilepsy. Then the shock was such that it sickened me even to make a movement, and nothing would have pleased me better than never to have wakened again. At present this *horror of life* is less strong already and the melancholy less acute. But of *will* I have none, of desires hardly any or none, and of everything belonging to ordinary life, the desire for instance to see my friends, although I keep thinking about them, almost none. That is why I am not yet at the point where I ought to think of leaving here, I should have this depression anywhere.

And it is only during these very last days that my repulsion for life is in any way radically modified. From that to will and action there is still some way to go.

It is a pity you are always condemned to Paris and that you never see the country except again what lies round Paris. I think it is not more unfortunate for me to be in the company I am in, than for you to have always the inevitable Goupil & Co. From this point of view we are fairly equal. For in your case it is only in part that you can carry out your ideas. However, once we have got used to these annoyances, it becomes second nature.

I think that though the pictures cost the canvas, paint, etc., nevertheless at the end of the month it is more profitable to spend a little more in this way and make use of what after all I have learnt, than to abandon them, since anyhow you have to pay for my keep. And that is why I am doing it; thus this month I have four canvases of 30 and two or three drawings.

But the money question, whatever we do, remains still the chief enemy, and we cannot deny or forget it. As much as anyone could in this respect I remember my obligation. And perhaps I shall be able even yet to pay back all I have spent, for what I have spent I consider as taken if not from you at least from the family, so consequently I have produced some pictures and shall do more. That is to act as you yourself are acting too. If I were a man of property perhaps my mind would be more at liberty to work at art for art's sake, now I content myself with thinking that by working industriously, even without thinking of it, I may perhaps make some progress.

These are the colours I need:
3 emerald green
2 cobalt
1 ultramarine
1 orange lead (big tubes)
6 zinc white
5 metres of canvas

Thanking you for your kind letter, I grasp your hand, your wife's as well.

Yours,
Vincent.

Leighton appeals to an old friend

The only President of the Royal Academy to be ennobled by Queen Victoria for his services to art was Frederick Leighton. He worked hard at representing artists' interests, work which was possibly a cause of the heart disease which in 1895 became so threatening that his doctors advised rest. At that moment, the annual Academy Banquet was in prospect, so someone had to take his place to preside; Leighton decided to appeal to Millais, who had come to visit him with fellow Royal Academicians just before this letter was written. Millais accepted the invitation. Leighton left for Algeria to rest, but died early in 1896.

(to John Everett Millais)[11] The Athenaeum, Pall Mall, S.W.
March 27th, 1895, 9.45 p.m.

Dear Millais,
Fresh from the meeting and your touching and affectionate expressions, I write a little word which may at first startle you, that you must not answer at once, and that you cannot push away.

My dear old friend, there is *only one man*, whom *everybody*, without exception, will acclaim in the chair of the President on May 4th – a great artist, loved by all – *yourself*. You will do it admirably, that I well know; and you will have the huge advantage of doing it once only instead of year after year. You have a misgiving about your voice; but, in the first place, it is only *at first* that your hoarseness hinders you; your voice warms as you go on; and in the second, it is *quite immaterial whether you are heard all over the room*. Those nearer will hear and enjoy you; the rest may be read, as the whole English-speaking world will read in the columns of the *Times* (the reporter is at your elbow, and you will give him your MS.) what you say on this occasion.

Dear Millais, every man in the profession will rejoice to see you in that chair on that night; and let an old friend of forty years say you *may* not refuse this honour. You said very kindly just how that all my brothers would come to my aid at this juncture. I ask you, in full confidence, to do so.

Ever yours affectionately, Fred. Leighton.

The Millais-nium

Millais succeeded Leighton as President of the Royal Academy, to the great pleasure of many colleagues. Here is one of the letters of congratulations which flowed in.

(to John Everett Millais)[12] Draycott Lodge, Fulham S.W.
February 24th, 1896

My dear Millais,

I don't know whether it is definitely settled yet that you shall be the President of the Royal Academy, but I have no doubt that it soon will be, for, whatever differences of interest there may be among the members, when once it was known that there was a possibility of your accepting the post, there could have been, and there will be, but one feeling about the surpassing fitness of the choice of yourself . . .

That you may hold it for some years is my hearty wish, but I trust that you will not make any kind of promise to keep it for life. The post is quite a different thing to fill, in the amount of work required, to what it was in Sir Joshua Reynolds' time. London, with its six million of inhabitants, and about three-quarters of these calling themselves 'artists', would wear any man to death if he felt there were no escape for him. It would assuredly interfere with his opportunities for work very mischievously. I was sorry that so true an artist as Leighton allowed himself to be hampered with the duties permanently . . . He did the duties magnificently, but he could have worked magnificently also, and the work would have remained for all generations; and this may be the same with you.

Give my felicitations to Lady Millais, who will have to take so large a part in the new honour; and give my love to Mary.

Yours very affectionately
W. Holman Hunt

Did you hear of Lear's pun? – which would be more appropriate now. It was – that the *Millais-nium* of Art had come. You have gone a letter higher – from P.-R.B. to P.R.A.

The century ended according to the calendar in 1900. That year saw Henry Adams in Paris at the Universal Exhibition looking for a symbol to stand for the new epoch, as the statue of the Virgin Mary had symbolised the Middle Ages. He chose not a work of art, but the dynamo. This prescient choice aptly embodied the extent and pace of change which would be brought forward by the new century, while its mechanical character sadly strengthens the views of those historians who end a long century at the beginning of the Great War in 1914. With the twentieth century's changes, the arts have continued to transform themselves; all the circumstances of an artist's life we have followed through the nineteenth century such as training, patronage, exhibitions and travel have taken on different characteristics.

Letters, though, have continued to be written. They are now supplemented for the historian by many other sorts of record including sound archives, films and videos. Telephone conversations more rarely leave a trace, so here we are still lacking information as we do about conversations in past ages. Also, telephone talk is at a distance, which makes the loss rather substantial. The telephone, however, has not superseded the mail; both are needed. A choice of means can be a matter of temperament; conference makes a ready man, Bacon says, here is your born telephonist; writing makes an exact man, the letter writer and now the user of electronic mail. The anthologist of artists' letters for the twentieth century will not run short of material; some of the evidence is already in print, and how fascinating a fuller picture promises to be.

NOTES

CHAPTER ONE

1. Chesnau, pp. xiv, 75.
2. Hawthorne, pp 114, 123–4. The novel was published in 1859, but for its English edition the title was changed to *Transformations*.
3. Holt, pp 95–7. Peter von Cornelius (1783–1867) returned to Munich in 1819, where he painted frescoes of Greek gods and heroes in the new Glyptothek and a 'Last Judgement' in the Ludwigskirche. He became director of the Munich Academy in 1824, but went to Berlin in 1841 to work on a project for a Gothic cathedral which was not built. A cartoon for the proposed murals 'The Four Riders of the Apocalypse' was the significant outcome of this project.
4. Visconti, pp xxi-xxii. Antonio Canova (1757–1822) was born in Venice but his career centred on Rome. A major commission was the monument for Pope Clement XIV (completed in 1787) but he was also well known for graceful single figures and groups of subjects such as Cupid and Psyche, or the 'Three Graces' (a version of which was jointly bought in 1994 by the Victoria and Albert Museum and the National Gallery of Scotland). He was in England in 1815 after a visit to Paris where Pope Pius VII had employed him to recover works of art taken from the Vatican by Napoleon.
5. Cassirer, pp 290–1 (new translation). Anselm Feuerbach (1829–80) studied in Germany, and in Paris under Thomas Couture. His symbolist pictures of classical figures such as Medea and Iphigenia are leading examples of classical idealism in German painting. His work is well represented in German public collections, notably Berlin.
6. Delaborde, pp 113–4, 174–6 (new translation). Hippolyte Flandrin

(1809–64) and his brother Paul Flandrin (1811–1902) both succeeded in their chosen fields of religious painting and landscape. Hippolyte Flandrin was an active muralist in the 1840s and 1850s; the tally of his work in Paris includes Saint-Séverin, Saint-Germain-des-Prés, and Saint-Vincent-de-Paul, as well as Saint-Paul at Nîmes and Saint-Martin-d'Ainay at Lyon.

7. Bashkirtseff, p 199 ff, p 212 ff (American translation). Marya Bashkirtseva (1858–84) was born in Poltova, Russia, the daughter of a Count. She kept her diary in French from the age of fourteen, and it is a selection from this, published under the French version of her name that made her posthumously famous.

Her painting was in a realist style, and received some recognition at the Salon, even a commendation; but this was for a sketch she had hesitated about sending, and she was irritated that it had been given an award in preference to a more ambitious work. The ribbon was hung around the neck of the family's dog.

The translation of the Latin quotation is: 'the dignified house of literary studies, the home of the world's words, the fatherland of liberty'. Marie Bashkirtseff's mother's house was in the rue Ampère.

8. Lethève, p 16.

9. Millais, pp 13–14.

10. J. S. Mills, pp 223–5. Sir Hubert von Herkomer (1839–1914) began a successful academic career with a painting of Chelsea pensioners, called 'The Last Muster' (1857), but his more regular subject matter was working life, such as 'Hard Times' (Manchester) or 'Found' (Tate Gallery). A characteristic portrait is that of Admiral Lord Fisher in the National Portrait Gallery, London.

11. Colmjon, p 35. Gerard Bilders (1838–65), was born in Utrecht, the son of a painter. A patron paid for his art education at the Hague, where he became an early member of the landscape artists' group which became known as the Hague School. Anton Mauve, Vincent van Gogh's cousin, was a friend and contemporary. Bilders died of tuberculosis at the age of twenty-seven. His patron, J. Kneppelhout, published his letters in 1876.

J. H. Weissenbruch (1824–1903) was a senior member of the Hague school; Paulus Potter (1625–54) was a celebrated Dutch animal painter, and Jean-Antoine-Theodore, Baron Gudin (1802–80), was French.

12. Mackmurdo, pp 23–4. Selwyn Image (1849–1930) was ordained priest in 1873, but gave up his orders to become a professional artist. Stained glass design was one of his successful activities. He was accorded a cherished honour in 1910, the Slade professorship at Oxford. He was much in demand as a lecturer and took a broad view of art; in one of his letters he quoted with approval the view of Alfred Stevens, 'there is only one Art, and its name is Architecture, Painting, Sculpture, Metal-work, Embroidery, Pottery etc etc etc etc etc.'

13. E. Mills, pp 88–9. John Ruskin (1819–1900), at the time of his first encountering Frederic Shields (1833–1911) was one of the foremost English writers and lecturers on art, besides being concerned with the idealistic Guild of St George which he had founded. His early defence of Turner and of the Pre-Raphaelites had given him a distinctive role as a critic, which he enlarged by a wide knowledge of art, architecture and nature. The Pre-Raphaelite sincerity of Shields' work clearly impressed him. William Henry Hunt (1790–1864), nicknamed 'Bird's Nest Hunt' after his favourite subject, exhibited nearly eight hundred of his delicately stippled pictures at the Society of Painters in Watercolours during his career. Shields progressed from engraving to mural painting, of which his major achievement was the decoration of the Chapel of the Ascension, Bayswater Road, London, now destroyed.

14. Lecoq de Boisbaudran, pp 51, 55, 105 and 108. Horace Vernet (1789–1863) was born in the Louvre, the son of a painter, who made his reputation as a painter of battle pictures. From 1828 to 1835 he had been the predecessor of Ingres as director of the French School in Rome. His distinction and membership of the Institut gave his patronage real value in promoting a book.

Horace Lecoq de Boisbaudran (1802–1867) taught at the Ecole Royale de Dessin et de Mathématiques, founded in the reign of Louis XV, and of which he was the director from 1841 to 1849. The school's purpose was to train craftsmen and designers of ornaments; his pupils included Fantin-Latour, the sculptors Carpeaux, Dalou and Rodin, besides Alphonse Legros who subsequently taught in London at the Slade. Lecoq de Boisbaudran's system was based on drawing from memory, unlike the copying books he so much disliked.

15. Du Maurier, p 235. George du Maurier (1834–96) wrote this letter in the year which made a decisive break in his career by his accepting a staff position on *Punch*. His grand-daughter Daphne du Maurier wrote in her edition of his letters that this was the end of his ambition as a painter. He was a notable book illustrator, and published two novels as well as his major success *Trilby* (1894), the story of a singer under the influence of a mesmeric fellow musician, Svengali.

Frederick Walker (1840–75) benefited from the praise of Ruskin, became a successful black and white illustrator, but died young. Swinburne's *Faustine* was published in the first series of *Poems and Ballads* in 1866.

16. Pissarro, pp 294–5 (American translation). Camille Pissarro (1830–1903) arrived from the West Indies in 1855 in Paris, where he quickly became associated with innovative art. He showed work in the Salon des Refusés in 1863, and at the first Impressionist exhibition in 1874. Under the influence of his friendship with Seurat, he used a pointillist style for some years. Lucien

Pissarro (1863–1944) moved in 1890 to London. His books and paintings, especially of landscape, gave him a successful career.
17. Sweet, p. 23

CHAPTER TWO

1. Ruskin, p 194–6. *The Elements of Drawing* (1857) was a successful and influential publication, embodying as it did Ruskin's philosophical reflections about art and nature while at the same time giving practical advice. A rival book by C. R. Leslie, *A Handbook for Young Painters* (1855) is a contrast; it was based on Leslie's lectures at the Royal Academy where he was professor of painting, and had a more professional tone, with its chapters on composition and the choice of subjects, or the rules and practice of the schools, whether the old masters, Flemish and Dutch art or the British school.
2. Holt, pp 88–9. Carl Carus (1789–1869) published *Nine Letters on Landscape Painting* in 1831. He was a doctor and botanist whose interest in painting and drawing was for the sake of his natural history studies. Landscape for Carus was essential, while figures in painting were of secondary importance.
3. Holt, p 77, Philip Otto Runge (1777–1810) studied in Hamburg, Copenhagen, and after an interruption by the Napoleonic wars in Dresden. His mystical art, seeking a spiritual dimension through colour and form attracted the attention of Goethe who partially incorporated Runge's ideas in his theory of colour which he published shortly after Runge's death.
4. Friedenthal, vol. 2, p. 100.
5. Cassirer, pp 223–4 (new translation). Alfred Rethel (1816–59) worked as a historical painter in Frankfurt, where he painted murals for the Imperial Hall of the Romer, and in Aachen where he worked in the Council House. At Dresden there is a mural of 'Hannibal Crossing the Alps' (1842–4).
6. Leslie, pp 84–5. John Constable (1776–1837) is an artist whose work is mainly found in London. It is selectively represented in the National Gallery, more fully in the Tate Gallery, while the Victoria and Albert Museum was given by his daughter a splendid collection including small lyrical sketches and first versions of major works.
7. Goldwater and Treves, p 194. Alfred Sisley (1839–99) was a fellow student of Monet and Renoir in Gleyre's studio at the *Ecole des Beaux Arts*, specialising in landscape. He exhibited at the first Impressionist exhibition of 1874. Examples of his work are found in many galleries in Europe and America.
8. Holt, pp 470–1. George Seurat (1859–91) was the systematiser who turned the colour ideas of the Impressionists into a technique of dots, called divisionism or pointillism, adding to it a formal type of composition based on the Golden Section. His *Bathers at Asnières* is in London, *Sunday on the Island of*

La Grande Jatte is in Chicago. The term Neo-Impressionism was invented for him and his followers in 1886.

9. Holt, pp 479–80. Vincent van Gogh (1853–90) began his Parisian studies in 1886 in Cormon's studio, where his friends including Seurat and Gauguin induced him to lighten his palette. In 1888 he went to Provence where his most famous work was done. The largest holding of van Gogh's work is in the van Gogh Museum in Amsterdam, but there are works in galleries round the world.

Zouage de paix is Alphonse Daudet's patois version of *Juge de Paix*, that is to say 'Justice of the peace'.

10. Repin, vol 1, pp 240–1 (new translation). In 1876 Ilya Repin (1844–1930) and his family joined the artistic community of Abramtsevo, argued to have been the cradle of modern Russian art. Repin was a member of 'The Wanderers', the Realist group which aimed at bringing art to the people. His historical paintings are his major achievement, but he also painted portraits including Tolstoy's in 1887. Repin taught at St Petersburg from 1893 to 1907, but after the October Revolution in 1917 he retired to his estate in Finland.

11. Boethius, p 24. Anders Zorn (1860–1920) made his international reputation as an etcher of nudes and portraits; he was, however, also a skilful painter of Swedish rural life. The house he had built in Mora, his native town, was the focus of Zorn's celebrated hospitality to fellow artists and patrons. Today the house and an adjoining museum demonstrate both his versatility as an artist and his taste as a collector.

12. Friedenthal, vol 2, pp 25–7. Gottfried Schadow (1764–1850) became sculptor to the Prussian court in 1788, and director of the Berlin Academy of Arts in 1816. His most prominent public monument is the Quadriga of Victory for the Brandenburg Gate, Berlin.

A 'lay figure' is the term employed for a model, often of jointed wood, used as a guide by artists for poses, or as a stand on which to arrange clothes or drapery. Jupiter seduced Danae in the form of a shower of gold.

13. Carr, pp 37–9. Harriet Hosmer (1830–1903) received important public commissions, including a colossal statue of Thomas H. Benton for the state of Missouri, now in Lafayette Park, St Louis. It was partly through the large editions of smaller works, however, that she was popular. The reference to successful sculptors and their patrons are to Hosmer's master John Gibson (1790–1866), notorious for his 'Tinted Venus', and Bertel Thorwaldsen (1768–1844), a definitive collection of whose work is in the Thorwaldsen museum in Copenhagen. Gibson commented on his Venus that it was 'the most carefully laboured work I ever executed . . . I tinted the flesh like warm ivory scarcely red, the eyes blue, the hair blonde, and the net which contains the hair golden'.

14. Watts, vol 3, pp 62, 64–5. George Frederick Watts (1817–1904) studied

in Italy for three years (1843–6), returning to England to paint portraits and ambitious allegorical paintings of subjects like 'Hope' (several versions, one in the Tate Gallery). A gallery built at Compton, Surrey, has a major series of these allegories, and the National Portrait Gallery owns a good group of portraits.

15. Gauguin, pp 238–9 (new translation). Paul Gauguin (1848–1903) gave up stockbroking for art in 1883, when he moved to Pont Aven, Brittany, taking a leading role among the artists working there. His most individual work, though, was done in the South Seas, especially in Tahiti, where he first arrived in 1891.

16. Barrington, pp 215–6. Giovanni Costa (1826–97) was mainly a landscape and marine artist. The editor of this letter interpolated a note about Costa's own practice; 'he himself used for small studies the bottoms of the boxes in which Havannah cigars are imported, and which are made of cedar-wood'. The Latin quotation may be translated: (celebrating) 'in the greatest of joy, soul and body, with well-sounding cymbals'.

CHAPTER THREE

1. Andersson, p 65 (new translation). Karin Larsson (1859–1928) was a gifted painter who studied in Sweden and Paris before her marriage in 1883 to Carl Larsson (1853–1919). Her distinctive style of interior decoration for their house at Sundborn, Dalarna, was a landmark, still rightly admired by visitors today. The light colours were in sharp contrast with the gloomy, heavy interiors in fashion in Sweden in the 1890s. Karin Larsson was an expert weaver, embroiderer and designer, so that fine textiles are a feature of the house. In this extract from a letter, the other expected visitors mentioned, Eva Bonnier and her sister, belonged to the family which owned the publishing house of Bonniers; Karl Skredsvig was a Norwegian painter also working in France at that time.

2. Stanton, pp 353, 351, 342. Rosa Bonheur (1822–99) started exhibiting at the Paris Salon in the 1840s, but her major success 'A Horse Fair' was exhibited in 1853. Thenceforward she was one of the most celebrated European animal painters, with a circle of collectors in Britain and elsewhere. Her dealer Gambart promoted her work by exhibitions as far afield as America and Australia.

3. Modersohn-Becker, p 29, pp 78–9. Paula Becker's wealthy uncle Wulf von Bultzingslowen is here mentioned. When she first went to Worpswede she studied with Fritz Mackensen. She married Otto Mendelsohn in 1901.

4. Cassirer, pp 150–1 (new translation). Caspar David Friedrich (1774–1840) spent most of his career in Dresden, where he taught at the Academy. His romantic landscapes frequently include figures looking away from the spectator,

who thus can identify with the experience of the view. His work is best represented in Dresden.

5. Knowles, vol 1, pp 319–20. Johann Heinrich Füssli (1741–1825), who later anglicised his name to Fuseli, was born in Zürich, where he trained for holy orders. He exposed a dishonest magistrate and his career ended. On going to London, he was encouraged by Reynolds to become an artist, and then spent three years in Italy, making a particular study of Michelangelo. He returned to an artistic career in London where he taught at the Royal Academy, of which he became Keeper in 1804.

6. Whitley (1930), pp 154–5. Thomas Bewick (1753–1828) is celebrated for his two major publications, the *History of Quadrupeds* (1790) and the *History of British Birds* (1797–1804). His technique of wood engraving was exceptionally fine, since he used the end grain, not the side of boxwood. A variety of swan is known in his honour as Bewick's Swan.

7. Beckett, pp 329–30, 333, 336, 340. This is John Constable's writing *verbatim*, unaltered by his biographer C. R. Leslie. John Tinney's picture was 'Stratford Mill', and Arrowsmith was the dealer who sold Constable's pictures in Paris.

8. Gage, p 120. J. M. W. Turner (1775–1851) has the Clore Gallery at the Tate devoted to showing his *extraordinary* oil paintings, and there are a selected number of his works in the National Gallery, one of which he bequeathed with the proviso that it should be hung next to a Claude. His outstanding gifts as a watercolourist can be seen from time to time in shows drawn from private and public collections, of which the most important is that in the British Museum.

Sir Francis Chantrey (1781–1841) was one of the main English portrait sculptors of the day, who bequeathed money to the Royal Academy for the purchase of 'works of art of the highest merit . . . executed in Great Britain', a bequest still in existence. Lord E. is the Earl of Egremont, one of Turner's best patrons, in whose house at Petworth, Sussex, Turner stayed and painted a number of major works.

9. Knox, p 58. Ellen Sharples (1769–1849) emigrated with her husband James Sharples to America, where she practised as a portrait artist. After her husband's death she returned to England and lived in Bristol.

10. Layard (Keene), pp 186–8. Charles Keene (1823–91) worked as an illustrator throughout his career, and as a cartoonist for *Punch* from 1851.

11. Mrs G. Burne-Jones, vol 2, p 231. 'Merlin and Nimue' is in the Lady Lever Art Gallery, Port Sunlight, and 'The Merciful Knight' is at Birmingham.

12. Manning, p 125. Sir Hamo Thornycroft (1850–1925) received many public commissions for historical and commemorative subjects, including statues of Queen Victoria in England and India. The statues of King Alfred in Winchester and of Cromwell outside the Houses of Parliament are by him.

13. Cassirer, p 338 (new translation). Adolf Menzel (1815–1905) was perhaps

the most distinguished German book illustrator of the century. He also painted a series of oil paintings of the age of Frederick the Great in addition to his illustrations.

14. Haydon, vol 1, pp 426–7. Benjamin Haydon (1786–1846) had the ambition but not the good fortune to become a major painter of historical subjects. He was active in public life, influencing the public purchase of the Elgin Marbles and successfully advocating a public competition for murals in the Houses of Parliament, rebuilt after the fire in the 1840s.

15. Toulouse-Lautrec, p 12. Count Henri de Toulouse-Lautrec (1864–1901) quickly made a reputation as a poster artist in the 1880s; his sense of line and flat surface made him well suited for lithographic design. An early riding accident prevented his legs from growing, and alcoholism contributed to his early death.

CHAPTER FOUR

1. Zola, p 279–80.

2. Layard (Lawrence), pp 161–2. Joseph Farington (1747–1821) was a landscape artist in oils, but also an active topographer who published the results of his sketching tours. His protégés included John Constable who took his London house in Charlotte Street after his death.

3. Friedenthal, vol 2, pp 62–4. Theodore Géricault (1791–1824) was as impatient of classical teaching as his friend Delacroix. After the controversial reception of his 'Raft of the Medusa' he made a stay in England. He found horses and racing attractive subjects; he was also shocked by poverty in London, a subject he illustrated in lithographs. He returned to France in 1822, where he died two years later.

4. Whitley (1930), pp 143–4.

5. Butler, pp 107–9. Elizabeth Thompson (1850–1933) and the poet Alice Meynell were sisters, brought up in Italy by their father who tutored them. Elizabeth is better known by her married name as Lady Butler. The instant fame recorded in this letter was for her picture 'The Roll Call', a group of the survivors from an engagement in the Crimean War, not specified by the artist; while it is sometimes described as Inkerman, this battle was fought in the autumn, before there was snow on the ground, so it is perhaps better to think of the picture as symbolic of the soldiers' suffering. There are several references in the letter to the heroic but tragic charge of the misdirected Light Brigade into a Russian gun position at Balaclava. 'The Roll Call' was the artist's second Royal Academy picture, and her career never looked back. Galloway was the name of the Manchester collector who first bought the picture, while the Agnews were members of the family which still has premises in Old Bond Street, London.

6. Millais vol 1, p 342-3, 346. Sir John Everett Millais (1829–96) was born in Guernsey, with such natural talent that he was accepted at the Royal Academy Schools at the age of eleven. He formed an alliance with Holman Hunt and Rossetti which they called a Pre-Raphaelite Brotherhood, a target for press attacks, though Ruskin defended them. Millais' career at the time of this letter was poised to take him forward to greater fame and eventually the Presidency of the Royal Academy.

John Leech (1817–64) was a prominent *Punch* artist. Tom Taylor was a barrister and writer, who wrote on art and edited several books, including Benjamin Haydon's memorial volumes.

7. Friedenthal vol 2, pp 133–5. Auguste Renoir (1841–1919) studied under Gleyre in 1862, and exhibited with the Impressionists in 1874. But he also showed at the Salon, partly because portraiture continued to have importance to his career. His later years were blighted by arthritis, but he nevertheless managed to supervise sculpture. The film director Jean Renoir wrote an affectionate memoir of his father.

8. Lucas vol 2, pp 346–7. Edward Austin Abbey (1852–1911) settled in England in 1878, where he became a successful illustrator and muralist. A major set of decorations is in the Public Library at Boston, Massachusetts, on the theme of 'The Holy Grail.'

9. Whitley (1928), pp 150–1. Sir Thomas Lawrence (1769–1830) had his own studio for portraits in Bath at the age of twelve, painted Queen Charlotte at twenty, and became the main English portraitist of his day. Part of his royal commission for portraits in the Waterloo Chamber at Windsor Castle is also documented in this book. Lawrence became President of the Royal Academy in 1820.

10. Haydon vol 2, pp 120–1. Haydon's painting 'The Mock Election' remains in the Royal Collection. The artist's friend was General Sir Thomas Hammond. Mr Seguier was a prominent figure in the art world, an adviser to Sir Robert Peel and George IV, director of the British Institution, was appointed as the first Keeper of the National Gallery.

11. Friedenthal, vol 2, pp 110–11. Jean-François Millet (1814–74) settled in Barbizon in 1848, where he painted rural subjects such as those described in this letter. His slow recognition only became public after the Paris exhibition of 1867. Thoré–Burger was a critic who wrote about Millet's work; Martinet was the name of the dealer at whose gallery the paintings were shown.

12. Pissarro, pp 22–3 (American translation). Heymann was a dealer who showed Pissarro's work; his business had been affected by the financial problems of France in the late 1880s, the many causes of which included agricultural depression, the high prices of imported raw materials, and competition from mass market products for traditional French luxury goods. Georges Petit was another dealer, while Félix Bracquemond was a colleague, rich enough to buy

his friends' work, which he bequeathed to the Louvre. At this date Pissarro was working in a pointillist style, which is what he means when he refers to 'our common struggle'.

13. Rouart, pp 153–4. Berthe Morisot (1841–95), a grand-daughter of Fragonard, was one of the Manet circle, who married Eugène Manet. She sat for his brother Edouard, for example as one of the two women in 'The Balcony'. She here mentions two dealers, Durand-Ruel and Goupil (the firm for which Theo van Gogh worked); Mallarmé was a friend of the Manets, and in one of her letters Morisot describes how she was invited to one of the poet's Tuesday evening parties, but since they were normally restricted to men, she declined. Mme Hoschedé was Claude Monet's future second wife.

CHAPTER FIVE

1. Knox, pp 12–13.
2. Beckett, vol 2, pp 189, 195.
3. Erpel, p 63.
4. Carr, pp 263–4.
5. Reynolds, pp 288, 283, 279. Frank Holl (1843–88) was the son of an engraver, Francis Holl. His early career was as an illustrator for the *Graphic*, but he also painted on a large scale and was a successful portraitist. His best known picture is 'Newgate – Committed for Trial' at the Royal Holloway College, Egham, Surrey.
6. O'Driscoll, p 67. Daniel Maclise (1806–70) was born in Cork, Ireland, but made his career in London. In the 1830s he sketched contemporaries for *Fraser's Magazine*, and his book illustrations include works by Tennyson and Dickens. He scored a particular success with murals in the House of Lords, still in place, 'The Meeting of Wellington and Blücher at Waterloo' (1861) and 'The Death of Nelson' (1864).
7. Newton, p 163–4. James Abbott McNeill Whistler (1834–1903) was a military cadet at West Point, then a draughtsman for the Coast Survey before leaving the United States of America to study painting in Paris under Gleyre. Whistler moved to London in 1863 where he practised as a portraitist, besides experimenting effectively with pictures of the sea and the River Thames.

   Other people mentioned in this letter are Mme de Montebello, a neighbour in the building where Whistler had borrowed studio space, arranged by the Spanish painter La Gandara, and Mrs Whistler's sister Edith Burnie Philip (Bunnie). Binkie was a pet name for Whistler's wife, and Wam a pet name he used to refer to himself. *Obi*, an African term current in the West Indies, refers to superstition.
8. Layard (Lawrence) pp 105–7, pp 108–11. Claremont was the name of the royal residence. Mrs Wolff, who had separated from her husband, was one of

Lawrence's close circle, and his portrait of her, now in Chicago, he considered to be one of his best performances. He was rather slow about finishing it, and had to be prompted; but that was not unknown for Lawrence. One story goes that he met a client whose commission of a picture of his wife and son had remained unfinished; the artist said that he would be able at last to complete the picture of the mother and her baby. 'My wife,' was the reply, 'will be pleased to sit for you, but the baby is in the Guards'.

Edmond Hoyle was the author of a book of rules for games in print throughout the nineteenth century and even today available in an updated edition. Hoyle's *Short Treatise on Whist* was published in 1742, and his definition of that game's *Laws* were current from 1760 to 1864.

9. Manning, pp 32–5. Thomas Thornycroft (1815–85) and his wife Mary Thornycroft (1814–95) were both sculptors, and as the letter shows, in favour with Queen Victoria. A version of Marocchetti's statue was subsequently placed outside Westminster Hall. Thornycroft's sculpture was never cast as a public monument.

CHAPTER SIX

1. Friedenthal vol 2, pp 21–2. John Trumbull (1756–1843) served as a colonel in the American War of Independence, commemorated in his war paintings such as 'The Battle of Bunker's Hill'. He studied under Benjamin West from 1780 in London, where he remained until 1789. He was Ambassador in London from 1794 to 1804. The paintings mentioned in this letter were four large historical murals for the Rotunda of the Capitol in Washington, which had been damaged by the British and Canadian expedition in 1814.

2. Haydon vol 1, p 386–8. The conference was to be on the subject of the independence of Belgium, which the countries mentioned eventually agreed in 1839. A truce between Holland and Belgium was made in 1833.

3. Joubin, vol 1, pp 19–21 (new translation). Eugène Delacroix (1798–1863) received important public commissions in Paris especially from the 1840s; this particular decoration was the prelude to more work in the Chamber of Deputies and the Senate.

4. Chu, pp 355–6. Gustave Courbet (1819–77) had a growing reputation in the 1860s as a realist, which as this letter shows, was endorsed by the approval of the younger German artists.

Chenavard was an allegorical painter who had been responsible for a scheme of decoration for the secular Panthéon in Paris; but before painting began, a political change altered the building back into a church. Chenavard, Charles Blanc and Couder were admirers of the classical work of Cornelius, Kaulbach and Moritz von Schwind, which, as Courbet writes, had fallen out of fashion with a new generation.

5. Friedenthal vol 2, p 140. The reputation of Auguste Rodin (1840–1917) was at stake for this commission. It was not in fact installed as he wished, but he won the argument about the composition. His sculpture is especially well studied in the Musée Rodin, Paris.

6. Haydon, vol 1, pp 301–3. Sir David Wilkie (1785–1841) studied in Edinburgh, but the success of 'A Village Politician' (1806) led him to settle in London. He specialised in pictures of everyday life, but he also practised as a portraitist and as a historical painter. In 1840 he died at sea, an event magisterially commemorated by Turner in an elegaic painting 'Burial at Sea' (Tate Gallery).

7. Spencer, p 322. The Freer Gallery in New York continues to hold the pictures mentioned in this letter. Charles Lang Freer (1856–1919) maintained his friendship with Whistler from 1890 to the artist's death. Freer's other collecting passions, to which he devoted himself after retiring in 1900, were for oriental ceramics and painting, which he saw as complementary to his Whistlers.

The 'Cigale', a portrait of a young girl, translates as grasshopper. The butterfly was Whistler's own emblem, which he used to sign pictures and prints. Count Robert de Montesquiou chose the bat as his emblem.

8. Lethève, p 163.

9. Beckett, vol 4, p 325.

10. Lethève, p 163.

11. Keynes, p. 867.

12. Cassirer, pp 207–8 (new translation). Johann Christian Clausen Dahl (1788–1857) was a landscape painter with a special interest in effects of light and atmosphere, and like John Constable made studies of clouds, carefully observed and with scientific accuracy in mind. Dahl's existing appointment was at the Academy at Dresden.

13. Sikes, p 131. William Hazlitt (1778–1830) turned his early failure as an artist to some practical account in art criticism, but his main work was as a political journalist, literary critic and biographer.

14. McCoubrey, pp 56–7. Samuel Morse (1791–1872) although a founder of New York's National Academy of Design (1826) turned to the study of chemistry and electricity. He thought of the idea of a magnetic telegraph in 1832; in 1844 the first message, 'What hath God wrought' was sent over the experimental line between Washington and Baltimore. The Morse alphabet was devised for use in the telegraphic system.

15. Hutchins, pp 112–13. Randolph Caldecott (1848–86) was the author as well as the illustrator of a popular series of children's books which he began to publish in 1878. As we see here, he also illustrated other authors' books, and he contributed to magazines including *Punch* and the *Graphic.* At this date photographically prepared process plates were becoming more often used

instead of wood engraving for book illustration; unluckily the results in *Daddy Darwin's Dovecot* were uneven in quality, due to poor etching and faulty electrotypes.

CHAPTER SEVEN

1. Joubin, vol 1, pp 76–7.

2. Haydon vol 1, pp 148–50. Sir Charles Lock Eastlake (1793–1865) made a successful debut with paintings of Napoleon as a prisoner of war on H.M.S. Bellerophon (one is now in the National Maritime Museum). His more lasting reputation, however, is as a connoisseur and writer on art; his *Materials for the History of Oil Painting* was published in 1847, and he directed the fortunes of the National Gallery from 1855. Confusingly, his nephew Charles Locke Eastlake (1836–1906) was also a writer on art and a Keeper, though not the Director of the National Gallery; his best remembered work is *Hints on Household Taste* (1868).

A contemporary of Bartolommeo Ammanati (1511–92) shared Eastlake's distaste for the Neptune fountain, exclaiming 'Ammanati! Ammanati! What fine marble you have ruined!' The *palle* (balls) are insignia of the Medici.

Lord Exmouth was the commander of an English and Dutch fleet which in 1816 bombarded Algiers for nine hours; the Turkish Dey gave in to international insistence that the treaty abolishing Christian slavery should be enforced.

3. Stanton, pp 134–5.

4. Friedenthal vol 2, pp 118–20. Edouard Manet (1832–83) was a respected figure for the Impressionists, who much admired him. In this letter he is writing to a friend nearly a decade before the first Impressionist exhibition. Henri Fantin-Latour (1836–1914) is known for his still life and flower painting, but he was also a portraitist and painter of figure subjects.

A *chiqueur* works from memory, not a model; the actor's picture mentioned by Manet is of Pablillos de Vallodid, a court jester; 'Las Meninas' means Maids of Honour.

5. Repin, vol 1, pp 71–75. The artists of the day assessed by Repin include Jan Matejko (1838–93), the dramatic painter of Polish history, and the Munich artist Karl de Piloty (1836–86).

6. Friedenthal vol 2, pp 59–61. Paul Gavarni (1801–66) worked for *Le Charivari* and *Les Gens du Monde* as a satirical illustrator. His visit to London in 1848 here documented was the occasion for some sombre drawings of misery and poverty which he published in *L'Illustration*. Gavarni was also an illustrator of books by authors including Balzac, and two books of his own drawings were published in 1848 and 1850.

The words 'ladies, gin, stout, mistress' in this passage were originally in English.

7. Lucas vol 1, pp 63–4, 208–9. Luke Fildes' 'Applicants to the Casual Ward' is at the Royal Holloway College, Egham, Surrey, part of the important gift of the founder, from which paintings by Constable and Turner have recently been sold. *The Deserted Village* by Oliver Goldsmith, which Abbey was planning to illustrate was originally published in 1770. Abbey's picture 'The Callers' was later retitled 'The Visitors'. The postscript to the letter was written from the library of the Reform Club, Pall Mall.

8. Stirling, pp. 191–2. The O'Gorman Mahon insisted on the unique title. John Adams-Acton (1831–1910) was a prolific portrait sculptor, responsible among other monuments for the figure of John Wesley in front of Wesley's Chapel, London, and the recumbent memorial figure of Cardinal Manning in Westminster Cathedral.

9. Legge, pp 115–16. A main theme of Sturge Moore's *Art and Life* (1910) is his reverence for Flaubert. The open landscape described as 'Puvis de Chavannes' refers to that painter's characteristic choice of scene.

10. Strachey vol 1, pp 39, 77, 273. Edward Lear (1812–88) was fortunate to attract the patronage of the 13th Earl of Derby (a title not to be despised; one heir to this title turned down the Kingdom of Greece; 'Do they not know I shall be Earl of Derby?'). Lear was originally commissioned to make drawings of rare animals and birds owned by the Earl, then turned to travel and topography. His lasting fame is from his limericks, verse and drawings which started as an amusement for the Earl's grandchildren.

11. Stewart, pp 188–90.

12. Ballantine, pp 80–2. David Roberts (1796–1864) was a master of topographical lithography, whose books of travel in the Near East are justly considered exemplary. His daughter Christine, seventeen when this letter was written, was staying with the Cooke family at Richmond while her father was away.

13. McCoubrey, pp 93–6. George Catlin (1796–1872) was eight years in his first campaign of recording American Indians in the Far West. The results are in the National Museum in Washington. Between 1852 and 1857 he travelled in South and Central America, later in Europe. His *Memoirs of the North American Indians* was published in two volumes in 1841.

14. Remington, pp 56–8, 190, 230–1. Frederic Remington (1861–1909) is known for his illustrations, both for articles and books mainly about life on the Plains, west of the Mississippi River. His paintings and sculpture were in a realist vein, like his illustrations. A major collection of his work is at the Remington Art Memorial, Ogdensburg, New York. Roosevelt returned from commanding the regiment he had raised for the Cuban war in 1898 to be

governor of the state of New York. He became President of the United States in 1901 on the assassination of William McKinley.

CHAPTER EIGHT

1. George, p 292. Sir Robert Peel was Prime Minister, although he was soon to be out of office.
2. Stewart, p 290–1.
3. Strachey vol 2, p 352. This was written from Lear's second house in San Remo. He had sold the first, which he had called Villa Emily after his friend Tennyson's wife, and this house was called Villa Tennyson. His projected illustrations for Tennyson's poems were never completed.
4. Chu, pp 601–2. The 'Portrait of Jo' in the National Museum, Stockholm, is generally thought to be the original version.
5. Whitley (1928), pp 238–9. Francesco Bartolozzi (1727–1815), a founder member of the Royal Academy of Arts in London (1769) was responsible for engraving the diploma for Royal Academicians, still in use. The design was by Cipriani. Bartolozzi was a prolific engraver in line and stipple, receiving royal as well as commercial commissions.
6. Richart, vol 1, p 213. Francisco Goya (1746–1828) was at the end of his long and distinguished career. His work is most fully seen in Madrid.
7. Schnapper, pp 280, 279. Jacques-Louis David (1748–1825) gained the *Prix de Rome* in 1774, was admitted to the Academy in 1780, and painted his landmark picture, 'The Oath of the Horatii' in 1784. He was from that time the leading neo-classical painter in France. He was a representative of Paris in the Convention, voted for the death of Louis XVI, and became director of the Revolution's fêtes. He was twice imprisoned, released in 1795, and painted 'The Rape of the Sabines' in 1799 (in the Louvre). In 1804 he was appointed Napoleon's court painter. This letter documents his unrepentant stance in exile.
8. Tripier le Franc pp 424–5 (new translation). Antoine Jean, Baron Gros (1771–1835) was a pupil of David. Gros gained fame as the recorder of Napoleon's battles, following these with historical subjects. As this letter shows, he was devoted to David and his reputation. Gros was disappointed by the reception of his later paintings and drowned himself in the River Seine.
9. Rouart, p 131.
10. Van Gogh, pp 332–9. The passage about 'Woman Rocking' is illustrated with a drawing which shows the picture between two paintings of sunflowers. The canvas size 30 was one of van Gogh's usual sizes for canvases. He refers to Jan van Goyen (1596–1656) in describing the landscape. The artists he mentions as having suffered from mental illness include one artist he particularly admired, Adolphe Monticelli. The painters' merchant and dealer Père

Tanguy stored pictures for artists. Robert Rey had been the doctor in charge at the asylum in Arles from which van Gogh moved to St. Rémy.

11. Millais, pp 315–6. Frederick, first Baron Leighton of Stretton (1830–96) studied in Germany and Italy. He began his successful English career with 'Cimabue's Madonna carried in Procession through Florence' in 1855. This was purchased by Queen Victoria and is on loan from the royal collection to the National Gallery. Leighton's Italianate style was popular in reproduction, and he was personally much liked by artists.

12. Millais, p 330. William Holman Hunt (1827–1910) was one of the original Pre-Raphaelites; many of his religious subjects were enhanced by visits to Palestine for authentic detail. His work is well represented in the Tate Gallery; two versions exist of his picture of Christ, 'The Light of the World', one at Keble College, Oxford and the other in St Paul's Cathedral, London.

BIBLIOGRAPHY

The books listed are those from which quotations have been taken or those from which texts have been newly translated. Anthologies which will be of interest to art students have been given asterisks, some of them including material other than letters; a few are additional to sources used for this book. Readers who would like to know more about the artists will often find that there are biographies available, and quite a number of the books here cited have been published in several editions.

In appropriate instances the list cites editors in preference to writers of letters, whose names are normally included in the titles of books.

Andersson, I. *Karin Larsson: Konstnär och Konstnärshustru*, Stockholm 1986

Ballantine, J. *The Life of David Roberts*, Edinburgh 1866

Barrington, Mrs. R. *The Life, Letters and Work of Frederick Leighton*, London 1906

Bashkirsteff, M. *Letters of Marie Bashkirsteff*, n.d. (an American edition)

Beckett, R. B. (ed) *John Constable's Correspondence, vol 2*, Suffolk Records Society, 1964

Beckett, R. B. (ed) *John Constable's Correspondence, vol 4*, 1966

Boethius, G. *Anders Zorn*, Stockholm 1954

Boisbaudran, L. de *The Training of the Memory in Art*, London 1911

Burne-Jones, Mrs. G. *Memorials of Edward Burne-Jones*, London 1904

Butler, E. *An Autobiography*, London 1922

Carr, C. *Harriet Hosmer: Letters and Memoirs*, London 1913

Cassirer, E. (ed) *Künstlerbriefe aus dem neunzehnten Jahrhundert*, Berlin 1915

Catlin, G. *Letters and Notes*, published by the author 1841

Chesnau, E. *Education of the Artist*, London 1886

Chu, P.t-D. (ed) *Letters of Gustave Courbet*, Chicago and London 1992

Colmjon, G. *The Hague School*, Rijswick 1951

Delaborde, H. (ed) *Lettres et Pensées d'Hippolyte Flandrin*, 2 vols, Paris 1865

*Denvir, B. (ed) *The Impressionists at First Hand*, London 1987

Du Maurier, D. (ed) *The Young Du Maurier: a selection of his letters*, London 1951

Erpel, W. (ed) Van Gogh Self-portraits, Oxford 1964

*Friedenthal, R. (ed) *Letters of the Great Artists*, 2 vols, London 1963

Gage, J. (ed) *Collected Correspondence of J. M. W. Turner*, Oxford 1980

Gauguin, P. *Lettres de Paul Gauguin à Georges-Daniel de Monfried*, Paris 1920

George, E. *Life and Death of B. R. Haydon*, London 1967

Gogh, V. van *Further Letters of Vincent van Gogh to his Brother 1886–1889*, London, Boston and New York 1929

*Goldwater, R. and Treves, M. *Artists on Art*, London 1947

Hawthorne, N. *The Marble Faun*, Ohio 1968 (original edition 1860)

Haydon, F. W. (ed) *Benjamin Robert Haydon: Correspondence and Table-Talk*, 2 vols, London 1875

*Holt, E. G. (ed) *From the Classicists to the Impressionists*, New Haven and London 1966

Hutchins, M. (ed) *Yours Pictorially: illustrated letters of Randolph Caldecott*, London 1976

Joubin, A. (ed) *Correspondence d'Eugène Delacroix*, vol 1, Paris 1935

Keynes, G. (ed) *The Complete Writings of William Blake*, London 1966

Knowles, J. *The Life and Writings of Henry Fuseli MA, RA*, London 1831

Knox, K. McC. *The Sharples*, New Haven 1930

Layard, G. S. (ed) *Sir Thomas Lawrence's Letter-Bag*, London 1906

Layard, G. S. (ed) *The Life and Letters of Charles Samuel Keene*, London 1892

Legge, S. *Affectionate Cousins*, Oxford 1980

Leslie, C. R. *Memoirs of the Life of John Constable*, London (Phaidon) 1951

Lethève, J. *Daily Life of French Artists in the Nineteenth Century*, New York 1972

Levey, M. *The Soul of the Eye*, London 1990

Lucas, E. V. (ed) *Edwin Austin Abbey*, 2 vols, London 1921

*McCoubrey, J. (ed) *American Art 1700–1960*, Englewood Cliffs 1965

Mackmurdo, A. H. (ed) *Selwyn Image Letters*, London 1932

Manning, E. *Marble and Bronze: the art and life of Hamo Thornycroft*, London 1982

Millais, J. G. *Life and Letters of John Everett Millais*, London 1899

Mills, E. (ed) *The Life and Letters of Frederick Shields*, London 1912

Mills, J. S. *Life and Letters of Sir Hubert Herkomer CVO, R.A.*, London 1923

Modersohn-Becker, P. *The Letters and Journals of Paula Modersohn-Becker*, Metuchen, New Jersey (Scarecrow Press) c. 1980

Newton, J. (ed) *Le Chauve-Souris et Le Papillon*, Glasgow 1990

O'Driscoll, W. J. *Daniel Maclise*, London 1871

Pissarro, C. *Letters to his son Lucien*, London 1980
Remington, F. *Collected letters*, New York 1994
Repin, I. E. *Selected Letters 1867–1930*, 2 vols, Moscow, 1969
Reynolds, A. M. (ed) *The Life and Work of Frank Holl*, London 1912
Richart, J. G. y *Goya*, 2 vols, Barcelona n.d.
Rouart, D. *Correspondence of Berthe Morisot*, London 1957
Ruskin, J. *The Elements of Drawing*, London 1860
Schnapper, A. *David*, New York 1980
Sensier, A. *J. F. Millett*, Paris 1881
Sikes, H. M. (ed) *The Letters of William Hazlitt*, London 1979
Spencer, R. (ed) *Whistler*, New York n.d.
Stanton, T. (ed) *Reminiscences of Rosa Bonheur*, London 1910
Stewart, J. (ed) *Letters of Eugène Delacroix 1813–1863*, London 1971
Stirling, A. M. W. *Victorian Sidelights: from the papers of the late Mrs. Adams-Acton*, London 1954
Strachey, Lady (ed) *Letters of Edward Lear*, 2 vols, London 1907, 1911
Sweet, Frederick A. *Miss Mary Cassatt; Impressionist from Pennsylvania*, Norman, 1966
Toulouse-Lautrec, H. de *Unpublished Correspondence*, London 1969
Tripier le Franc, J. *Histoire de la vie et mort du Baron Gros*, Paris 1880
Tuer, A. W. *Bartolozzi and his Works*, London 1882
Visconti, E. Q. *The Elgin Marbles*, London 1816
Watts, M. S. *George Frederick Watts*, vol 3 (his writings), London 1882
*Whitley, W. T. *Art in England 1810–1820*, Cambridge 1928
*Whitley, W. T. *Art in England 1821–1837*, Cambridge 1930
Zola, E. *His Masterpiece*, London 1887 (original French edition *L'Oeuvre*, Paris 1886)

Index